Understanding the
German Shepherd Dog

Understanding the German Shepherd Dog

John Cree

The Crowood Press

First published in 2000 by
The Crowood Press Ltd
Ramsbury, Marlborough
Wiltshire SN8 2HR

British Library Cataloguing-in-Publication Data
A catalogue record for this book is available from the British Library.

ISBN 1 86126 342 2

Dedication
To Quest, the German Shepherd who introduced us to the breed. And to all
the other Shepherds who have filled or touched our lives during those happy
years of involvement. Who could ask for better companions?

Frontispiece: Ceilidh, from an original watercolour by Carol Bramley.

Photographs by J. Cree and A. Mollison, except where stated otherwise.
Line-drawings by Annette Findlay.

Throughout this book, 'he', 'him' and 'his' have been used as neutral pronouns.

Edited and designed by OutHouse Publishing Services,
Shalbourne, Marlborough, Wiltshire SN8 3QJ

Printed and bound in Great Britain

Contents

Acknowledgements

I am indebted to my family, and to various German Shepherd owners, for confirming the details of many of the anecdotes that I have used in this book.

My thanks are due to the Natural History Museum for permission to reproduce (in Chapter 1) details relating to the work of Francis Galton, taken from *A Natural History of Domesticated Mammals* by J. Clutton-Brock, and also to Brian Wootton for permission to quote (in Chapter 2) details from his book *The German Shepherd Dog* (see Further Reading).

I am grateful for the assistance given by those involved in the various photographic sessions, in particular to Alex Mollison for his dedicated work with his digital camcorder, which gave us fascinating action shots. His patience also resulted in a selection of transparencies for the jacket.

My thanks also to Irene, my wife, for her assistance in producing the manuscript.

Preface

Is your dog an ambassador for the German Shepherd breed? I should hope so – he or she may be just a lovable character who is your constant companion or a top-winning show specimen, it does not matter. He could be a police dog, or in the amateur field of Working Trials, Obedience or Agility, but whatever he is, your German Shepherd should still be considered by the people who meet him to be a good ambassador for our breed. We should all be looking to the general public for commendations on our dogs in general behaviour.

German Shepherds are not normally recognized as being outgoing towards strangers and in fact most strangers can be a bit cautious of Shepherds which are allowed the freedom to go and investigate people at will. Unfortunately, the reactions of some of these strangers sets off

W.T.Ch. Quest of Ardfern C.D.Ex. U.D.Ex. P.D.Ex. T.D.Ex.

Heldrews Forgive 'N' Forget of Ardfern C.D.Ex.

an uncharacteristic reaction from the dog and in consequence, creates the impression of a windy or aggressive representative of the breed. Things can go wrong and unexpected situations can create false impressions. These impressions stick in the minds of the people affected and probably in the minds of others when these events are relived with the appropriate exaggerations.

The creation of ambassadors can be easy or difficult to accomplish and this may depend on a variety of factors, but this reputation could easily be damaged or lost through an unfortunate and unexpected incident. Two principal factors help to create good ambassadors for the breed, they are breeding and environment.

Breeding does not have to come from top-class show stock or from the most successful breeding kennels. They may be able to supply a handsome dog but the background to their breeding programme may not take into consideration the requirements for work or the pet dog owners. Every German Shepherd that lives at home, no matter what his show or working potential, is a pet dog who meets and mixes with the general public.

Even show dogs that are normally kenneled will be produced in public from time to time to carry out their function in life – breed showing. They are on view to people, even those these people might represent only a limited section of the public, and they will do a great deal of harm to

Vikkas Electra of Ardfern C.D.Ex. U.D.Ex. W.D.C of Merit.

the breed if they do not have the character and socializing to create a favourable impression.

Breeding for character and temperament is important. Breeding from shy, aggressive or hyperactive stock may not result in disaster but is likely to require a lot more thought, conditioning and alertness to avoid the circumstances which could result in situations that may ruin much good work in overcoming the inbred handicaps.

Most puppies go into the hands of first-time buyers of the breed: they know the dog next door, down the street or at the other end of the village. He is a character, he loves fun and games, he is clever, and he never gets into trouble. The potential buyer has witnessed the life of the good ambassador of the breed and he wants one like it. This prospective buyer does not

know about the potentially shy, aggressive or hyperactive puppies which are available; only time and puppy development will bring him down to earth with the realization if he has been sold a 'pup'. On the other hand, ignorance, and at times over-protectiveness, on the part of the new owner can play its part in ruining a natural and potential ambassador.

The initial period of conditioning in a puppy's life, up to ten weeks of age, can create a sound foundation for the future or the complete lack of socialization can create many problems for the new owner.

The show puppy which is run on and does not make the grade can be a potential disaster when sold to an unsuspecting buyer. A lady came to a Working Trials meeting with an eight-month-old puppy from a very well-respected breeder. She

Tanfield Atholl of Ardfern C.D.Ex. U.D.Ex. W.D.Ex. T.D.Ex. (V Rated). (Photo. V. Oliver.)

had picked up the puppy three days earlier and it was the first time the puppy had been taken out of the breeder's kennels. She was everybody's friend, took to the lead without problems and was a super ambassador for the breed. However, this is not par for the course. All too often, I have had such puppies brought to my domestic training classes for socializing and to help overcome the various problems. Some of these youngsters cannot cope with the change of environment, some of the owners cannot cope. The result is disappointed owners who decided that this first venture into the world of German Shepherds is to be their last.

The German Shepherd is not a difficult breed to live with, he is a joy to have about the house. However, like many other breeds, a bad buy or a faulty upbringing can create the impression that the ambassador down the road is the exception to the rule rather than the character we are entitled to expect.

Breeders must keep in mind that although hip scores are important, so is character and temperament. Shape and construction are important – so is character and temperament. Size and movement are also important – so is character and temperament. The puppy you run on should have the lot – this is the breeding stock of the future – but it is equally important that the puppies that earn the hard cash which keeps the line going are the puppies that affect the opinions of the people who matter – the potential buyers of the future.

We must look after the German Shepherd pet dog owners, give them sound prospects as future ambassadors of the breed. Advise and help them to avoid problems or to cure them before they become ingrained into the dog's behaviour patterns. The first twelve months are particularly important. If we can help to achieve these aims the rescue units will find that their task is much less demanding.

John Cree, 1991

(Originally published in the *GSD League Handbook 1991* as an article entitled 'An Ambassador for the Breed'.)

Introduction

This book has been written for the German Shepherd Dog owner who wishes to live in harmony with his dog. It aims to help the owner know all about his own dog, to understand his character and to benefit from his companionship.

The German Shepherd's character is a combination of so many interacting ingredients that it can be difficult to assess which characteristics specifically influence the dog's outlook on life. Intelligence may be closely connected or combined with trainability. Steadiness of nerves may be the result of self-assurance; unwarranted aggression may also be related to self-assurance. Environmental conditions will also play a major part in forming the character of the German Shepherd Dog.

No two dogs are born with precisely the same character. Life's experience will broaden each dog's genetically inherited attitudes and responses. Although there are characteristics common to the breed, every German Shepherd Dog is unique; and it is important for any owner to believe there is no other dog like his own. As you read through this book, you might conclude that I consider the Shepherds I have owned to be something special. I would reply that any owner of a German Shepherd who does not think his dog is 'something special' does not deserve his company.

The strengths and weaknesses in an individual dog's inherited character will be influenced by his environment, from the earliest months of his life right through to the last. Even at eight weeks of age the environment can have some influence on a puppy's future. The longer the puppy remains in that environment before leaving for a new home, the more influential that period is. As the German Shepherd matures, other changes may take place, particularly if a bitch is spayed or a dog castrated, but the early months are crucial and a good inherited and environmental foundation is a key factor in ensuring that a German Shepherd Dog will live up to expectations.

Knowledge of the breed varies widely. Some German Shepherd owners can quote pedigrees, and appear to know the ancestry of every imported German-bred dog. There are breeders and show exhibitors who seem to know exactly how the dog should be constructed. There are those who train and work the breed professionally or for pleasure. Others know their dogs by having them share their daily lives in the home. And there are those who combine a number of these circumstances. Whatever the circumstances, real knowledge of a German Shepherd's character comes from training and living with him.

I make no attempt to study the characteristics associated with any specific line of breeding. The factors from line to line, and the changes in breeding that take place over periods of time, are highly variable. When we add the effect of the environment, I doubt if there is anybody sufficiently knowledgeable to give a valid and meaningful assessment of the effect of individual stud-dogs on the character of our breed. Certain stud-dogs have been a breeding disaster, leaving their progeny with inherited weaknesses in character; others have done the breed proud. But at the end of the day those factors can be overtaken by the generation that follows.

The dogs in our own household have been brought up with certain principles and standards in mind. This will obviously reflect in the character of our own dogs. The full environmental background of other dogs mentioned in this book is not always known, but I have included them because they help to illustrate the variations in the character of the breed. Where my own, or my family's, dogs are involved the anecdotes are accredited to the named Shepherds. However, where situations involving other dogs are described, some names have been changed to avoid any possible embarrassment to the owners.

Throughout the book, 'he' has been used as a neutral pronoun and therefore applies to both sexes. It would also be appropriate to refer to the breed as the German Shepherd (or simply Shepherd), just as in normal discussion.

CHAPTER 1

Character of the Breed

For German Shepherd Dogs there are three breed standards of any significance: German, British and American. Although the descriptive details may differ a little, the three are very similar in their interpretation. Rather than quote from one individual standard, this character description of the breed is based on a combination of the various attributes which make the German Shepherd so special.

General appearance helps to indicate the character of a dog. Strength, intelligence and suppleness should be apparent. Signs of vitality will be evident in his stance, movement, ear carriage and the sparkle in his eyes. There will be a visual indication of willingness, enthusiasm, courage and nobility. The sexual characteristics will be well defined. The masculinity of the males and the femininity of

Vicksburg Yalk's appearance signifies character and nobility. (Photo. V. Oliver.)

Duncan has an expression that typically denotes character.

the females should be obvious. Weak character, on the other hand, can show in a number of ways. A look in the eyes may indicate that the dog is troubled in mind, while a dog with his tail tucked between his legs may lack confidence and vitality.

An attractive appearance is desirable, but this must not be to the detriment of usefulness as a working dog. The intellect and character of the German Shepherd are ultimately more important than the finer points of construction and appearance. To win place tickets in the breed show ring is the worthy ambition of many, but this is pure personal vanity if breeding for such a purpose alone is at the expense

of the dog's character. A German Shepherd should not only look the part but should also be an enjoyable, well-behaved companion. Satisfaction between dog and owner should be obvious.

The future of the breed is dependent on its status as a companion of distinction or a highly valued working dog. It is perhaps as working dogs, whether for professional purposes or for competitive leisure activities, that German Shepherds best fulfil their true potential. A working dog's inherited attributes will have been stimulated by owners and handlers who fully appreciate the purpose for which they are bred.

As a puppy, Duncan was full of confidence.

It is unfortunate that the principal means of evaluating the quality of the German Shepherd is the breed show ring. 'Breed assessments' are occasionally carried out independently of shows, but it is the winners in the show ring that tend to become the mainstay of future breeding plans. During these evaluations or assessments, construction and general appearance are the principal characteristics under consideration. The 'character' of the dog is usually ignored, unless a significant fault is self-evident, such as an obviously shy or highly aggressive disposition. Certain judges may even ignore such behaviour if the dog has the construction and appearance of a winner.

Buying a pet German Shepherd with a long pedigree is no assurance that the dog will have the right qualities to fit into a domestic or working environment. I remember hearing of one very successful breeder/exhibitor some years ago who was asked, 'What consideration do you give to temperament?' The reply was, 'We have too many other things to think of to bother about temperament.' Although most breeders would not claim such an extreme view, there are still doubts about the priority some breeders give to the important character requirements that give the German Shepherd its distinctive qualities.

There is a case for arguing that Schutzhund training and the resultant qualifications are an indication of the inherited characteristics that control working ability. However, I do not believe the case is strong enough to have a mea-

Character – the essential elements

Temperament
Virtues
- Calm self-assurance
- Good sense, accompanied by spirit
- Ability to be at ease in company
- Ability to accommodate environmental experiences

Deficiencies
- Over-excitability or hyperactivity
- Nervousness or shyness
- Resentfulness or quick temper

Loyalty
Virtues
- Faithfulness and trust in the family
- Dependability and obedience
- Incorruptibility
- Ability to differentiate between friend and foe
- Submissiveness, coupled with the ability to apply respectful dominance

Deficiencies
- Perfidiousness
- Treacherousness
- Untrustworthiness

Intelligence
Virtues
- Quickness of understanding and power of reasoning
- Adaptability, tractability and trainability
- Result of the collective sum of all inherited elements of character

Deficiencies:
- Lack of imagination
- Indifference to constructive activities
- Weakness derived from a variety of inherited characteristics

Steadiness of nerves
Virtues
- Courage and ignorance of fear
- Confidence and defiance of recognized dangers
- Ability to counter aggression.

Deficiencies
- Aggressiveness or a tendency to bite
- Timidity or a tendency to skulk or sneak away in time of danger

Alertness
Virtues
- Attentiveness and observant awareness
- *Vigilance applied with all senses, even when resting*

Deficiencies
- Inactivity and a tendency to be detached
- Indifference to abnormal activities

Resilience
Virtues
- Good recuperative powers (physical and mental)
- Tirelessness in activity requiring mental as well as physical endurance
- Tenacity in reaching objectives

Deficiencies
- Fragility
- Irresolution and inability to persevere

Agilityand Suppleness
Virtues
- Muscular fitness
- Speed and nimbleness
- Co-ordination of movement; lack of 'stiltiness'

Deficiencies
- Lack of fitness
- *Inco-ordination of movement; clumsiness*

Scenting ability
Virtues
- Strength of olfactory nervous system
- Adaptability in use of scenting
- Willingness and ability to differentiate between different scents and odours.

Deficiencies
- Irresolution and lack of perseverance in applying scenting powers

Environmental (uninherited) influences
Virtues
- Sound general upbringing; good companionship
- Effective harnessing of specific inherited characteristics for special purposes
- Competent training and guidance for community life

Deficiencies
- Maltreatment, neglect or unwarranted isolation
- Tendency to turn virtues into vices

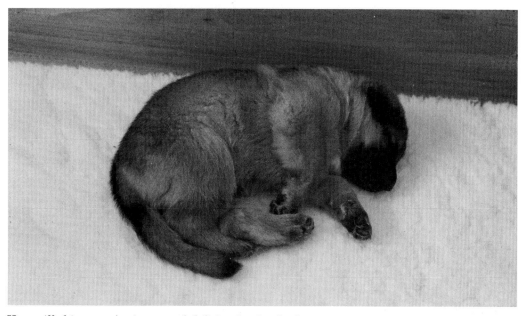

How will this puppy's virtues and deficiencies develop?

surable effect when breed judging gives such scant consideration to character and working ability. Choosing a dog for the competitive field of Working Trials, or for commercial activities such as police or security work, can be very difficult. When the working features of the breed are not being utilized to any great extent then assessment of these abilities for future breeding purposes becomes correspondingly diluted.

Overall, German Shepherds give great satisfaction as domestic pets. The suitability of German Shepherd puppies for the domestic market varies considerably, but the majority fit into a band of acceptability and become integrated unto community life without difficulty. However, a significant minority of puppies do require owners with knowledge and ability well above the norm, to understand the wider variations and inborn tendencies.

The character of the German Shepherd is a complex subject. Temperament is probably the principal feature which affects a dog-owner's life. Owners must understand the strengths and weaknesses of the dog's temperament before they can utilize or improve on nature's contribution. Shy and nervous puppies are an embarrassment and a danger to their owners, and breeders should consider them to be more than just a disappointment. Dogs with an excess of self-confidence which manifests itself as unwarranted aggression will do the reputation of the breed great harm unless the owner has the ability to influence and improve the dog's behaviour. Owners who lack the expertise to manage canine life and behaviour through to maturity can ruin the good work of a breeder who carefully studies breeding lines and produces well-balanced puppies.

The Tundra Wolf.

What is Character?

The character of the German Shepherd is made up of many interrelated characteristics This makes it difficult to define character, especially when some of these integral elements must be thought of in canine, rather than human, terms.

Does a courageous police dog think of the possible consequences when he attacks a man with a gun? Does a sheep worrier consider that his life is at stake because of such an enjoyable activity? These considerations go beyond the thinking of a dog. Without previous experience to guide him, a dog would not consider such situations to be dangerous. When trying to understand the working of a dog's mind, it is useful to have an appreciation of 'canine logic': 'A dog will always do what he considers to be in his best interest at that particular moment in time.' A dog's thinking is not governed by protocol or the laws of the land. We must judge the character of the German Shepherd on canine terms and not by human standards.

The character of the German Shepherd can be broken down into nine principal or lead characteristics. It is the interaction of any combination of these which results in a particular dog's attitudes and reactions. The varying strengths and weaknesses of these integral elements of character are such that every German Shepherd is unique, but certain defined patterns emerge. The box on page 16 should help owners to recognize the virtues and deficiencies of their own dogs.

The Golden Jackal.

The Coyote.

Historical Development of Character

The character of the German Shepherd is the result of thousands of years of development. The process of socializing and taming the progenitor of the dog began over 10,000 years ago, creating the basic inherited ingredients that have been moulded through centuries of selective breeding to give us the German Shepherd as we know it today.

It is important to understand the contributions that have been made over time in order to appreciate the dogs that live in our midst. The development can be classified in three stages:

1. Prehistoric development.
2. Domestication.
3. The German Shepherd Dog as a recognized breed.

Prehistoric Development

The wolf (*Canis lupus*) is known to be the principal progenitor of the dog (*Canis familiaris*). No doubt the coyote and the jackal played a marginal role in helping to formulate the variation in type. Dogs, wolves, coyotes and jackals have a number of characteristics in common, principally the number of chromosomes that make up their genetic profile: each has 78 chromosomes (39 pairs), and they can interbreed.

Eskimos in Canada crossed wolves with their own dogs to improve stamina. Wolves were also introduced into teams of sledge dogs. Today we find people breeding hybrids from wolves and German Shepherds. This in itself helps to confirm the origin of our own dogs.

There are variations in wolves throughout the world and no doubt they are all interconnected. It appears that various groups of dog breeds have evolved from these different types of wolf. The Eskimo Spitz dog originated from the American wolf, while the European Spitz dog probably comes from a mixture of the North American and European wolves. The herding breeds probably originated from a combination of the European and Indian wolves. The various continents knew no boundaries, and those adjacent to each other would create mixtures of types. It would appear that the herding, and therefore the shepherding, breeds are a group of dogs from one genetic source.

Throughout the ages, guarding was a feature that complemented the herding traits that early man utilized to maximum benefit in his efforts at animal husbandry. The wolf had the most promising background for development into a beneficial and practical companion for early man. Recognized as a carnivore, with a highly developed degree of intelligence, it succeeded as a group hunter that was able to live off prey much larger than itself. Today's North American wolf packs will tackle elk, caribou, moose or buffalo. Such animals are large enough to satisfy the hunger of a whole pack, including the wolves that are not fit to hunt, the old, infirm, nursing mothers, and juveniles not yet ready to learn the trade. Group hunting will not, however, prevent opportunism in the form of an individual wolf enjoying a snack of deermouse or snowshoe hare.

Co-operation and Organization

Much like human society, a wolf pack is held together in a hierarchy of dominance, submission, affection and fear. A proper pecking order is established, with the strongest-willed and fittest male or

The dominant and submissive poses that wild dogs will assume in order to communicate with each other are still apparent in the behaviour of today's domestic dog.

female applying the dominance required to achieve control within the pack.

Like present-day German Shepherds, each wolf would be unique in its character and its ability to contribute to the pack's activities. The principal activities would be hunting for food and protecting its own kind. Although the character of each wolf would be unique, certain defined patterns would emerge. As with the human race, some wolves would be born to lead and others born to follow, while others would like to lead but would be required to submit into an inferior role within the pack.

It would be difficult to assess the temperament of the wolf in today's conditions. The animals may well appear to be nervous or shy near humans. This could be due to their ability to 'accommodate environmental experiences'. Throughout the ages a pack of wolves, or a solitary one, would go for an easy kill to fill their stomachs. This may be a child or a domesticated animal. The wolf itself may have been on the menu for early man.

Loyalty to the pack and its leader was the foundation of the wolves' group system of existence, based on dominance, submission, affection and fear. The dominant leader carried the responsibility of managing the pack by applying his or her authority. This authority could only be gained by an ability to lead and ensure that food could be found. If this food was 'on the hoof', then the leader's guile, courage, intelligence and other lead characteristics would be tested in turning a mobile prey into a welcome meal.

Submission to the leader was vital to achieve reasonable harmony within a pack. It also created respectful affection. The challenge to leadership or the sorting of a pecking order down the line would be disruptive, and no doubt was from time to time. But the submissiveness of the majority of wolves to their leader is probably the most important factor in the domestication of the wolf into the human pack. It is very doubtful if potential leaders would integrate with human society. The ability of so many to submit to a leader certainly helped to make these animals an accepted addition to early life.

The submissive behaviour of the wolf would depend on the attitude of the more dominant animal, be it wolf or man. A very dominant attitude would result in a more subordinate and submissive response. If the more masterful authority was too tolerant without dominating, the subordinate wolf would try to assert himself. If the dominant party was over-aggressive in his domination, the subordinate and submissive wolf would be more likely to retreat through fear and become insecure within the pack. If the situation was bad enough, he may have found life on the outside of the pack more acceptable.

It was the wolf's intelligence, its power of reasoning and its adaptability, that helped it to achieve survival. Having the ability to take on prey larger than itself required the co-operation of the group. Some wolves with better scenting powers would detect a track or wind-scent the target. Others with good long-distance sight could spot movement at a distance and lead the pack to their quarry. The most

aggressive and courageous could then make the initial attack and immobilize the prey so that full bellies were assured for the whole pack. This ability to co-ordinate the strengths of the various individuals was an indication of the capacity and intelligence of wolves.

To tackle animals larger than themselves, even in the form of mob violence, took courage. No doubt there would be a number of wolves who would be happy to follow and give moral support. The animals who took the risk of a hoof in the ribs or skull, a slash from a set of antlers or being crushed by a fallen beast, had the fearlessness that ensured their position in the hierarchy of the pack.

The Senses
The alert and vigilant application of all senses would ensure that unwanted visitors were detected. The senses of smell and hearing would be of particular value. Again, with the prerequisite of locating their next meal, the alertness of these senses and of sight would be essential.

The tireless dedication to the search for food during hard times would be a drain on the wolves' mental and physical resources. The ability to travel some 20 miles (32km) or more in a day when following an injured target or a herd of caribou is only part of the story. The wolves' ability to attack and overcome powerful prey when their own lives were at stake shows just how tenacious and resilient they were.

Muscular fitness and co-ordination of movement gives the wolf the enduring gait that enables him to follow his prey for great distances. The ability to put on a turn of speed when required is essential if he is to catch his target. However, nimbleness is the factor that ensures his ability to twist and turn, so that even the most evasive creatures have difficulty in eluding this predator.

This is possibly one of the most important characteristics that ensured the survival of the wolf. Without an excellent sense of smell, wolves could not have detected distant prey. The invisible scent tracks that the wind carried from the hunted – body odour, and the scent of vegetation crushed by the animal's movements – would be a positive indication of a meal ticket at hand. To locate the ground scent of a passing animal would be important; but to determine the direction of the animal's movement would be vital to survival. For a wolf to follow the scent path in the wrong direction would end in failure, frustration and greater hunger.

Domestication

The environment of the time helped create the characteristics of the wolf and, therefore, the characteristics that were passed on to the domesticated species that preceded the dog. The arrival of man in their territories brought changes to that environment, and the wolves learned to accept these changes.

Wolves were probably hunted by man to feed his own family. Children would be considered as prey to an enterprising wolf. Yet, although man and wolf were living in conflict, man did learn to make use of wolf pups and secure a social bond with suitable animals as they reached maturity.

The domestication of various other species of animals was also taking place, for the prime purpose of supplying food: these were the forerunners of our present farm animals. Wolves began to be used to help with hunting, guarding and herding. The taming and training of wolves with selective breeding would prove to be a sig-

nificant advancement in the quality of early life. The development from wolves by selective breeding into early domesticated dogs was well established centuries before Roman times with the creation of three founder breeds: the hunting dog, the herding or shepherding dog and the guard dog.

The initial development of animal domestication may best be described by quoting from Francis Galton's writings (1865). Very briefly Galton states that there appeared to be six conditions under which wild animals could become domesticated.

1. They should be hardy.
2. They should have an inborn liking for man.
3. They should be comfort-loving.
4. They should be found useful to the savage.
5. They should breed freely.
6. They should be easy to tend.

The few animals that fulfilled all six conditions had been domesticated many centuries before. Any species which failed in one condition was destined to remain in its wild state.

It seems that very early social groups within the human race kept and brought up very young wild animals. These youngsters would probably have lost their mothers and would have died if not taken into an active community. They would be playthings for the children and would be looked after by the women. If these animals stayed within the community in adult life and bred under these circumstances so that future generations became dependent on man, these animals would be considered to be domesticated.

The six conditions quoted from Galton would have been essential attributes for a species to achieve full domestication. An expansion of these conditions will help with their understanding.

1. They should be hardy. A young animal has to survive removal from its own mother, probably before weaning, and must adapt to a new diet, a new environment, and new conditions of temperature, humidity, infection and parasitic infestation.
2. They should have an inborn liking for man. In present-day terms this means that the structure of the species has to be allied to that of man. It has to be a social animal whose behavioural patterns are based on a dominance hierarchy so that it will accept man as the leader and will remain imprinted on him in adult life.
3. They should be comfort-loving. Galton meant by this that the species must not be highly adapted for instant flight as, for example, many members of the antelope, gazelle and deer families. These animals will not feed or breed readily if constrained in a pen or herded too closely together.
4. They should be found useful to the savages. The primary function of captive animals to a primitive community is as an easily maintained source of food, a reliable larder that can provide meat when required. The selectively bred and domesticated dogs would fill this criterion by their ability to hunt with man and assist in providing meat for the larder.
5. They should breed freely. As Galton accurately observed, this is perhaps the most necessary factor for successful domestication, as can be seen from the difficulty of maintaining breeding colonies of many species in zoos, even

under the most favourable conditions that can be provided in captivity.
6. They should be easy to tend. This applies particularly to livestock, which must be reasonably placed, versatile in their feeding habits, and gregarious so that a herd or flock will keep together and can be easily controlled by a herdsman. Again, the selectively bred domesticated dog would have a role, by helping the herdsman to control, manoeuvre or guard the newly domesticated livestock.

It can now be seen how hunting, herding and guarding groups of dogs started to develop, each adapted to fulfil different functions in human communities. The continuation of selection would result in specialized breeds and the combination of requirements would encourage further specialization. This can be said of many herding dogs where guarding – the protection of a herd or flock against animal and human predators – also became a principal feature. Guarding also entailed defending the domestic abode and community compound, and giving warning of any danger.

The German Shepherd as a Recognized Breed

Sheep have been part of man's life for many centuries. They provided wool to clothe him and meat to sustain him. Specific types of dog were developed to help man with the flocks of sheep, either to control them when on the move or to contain them in an area for feeding or rest. The responsibilities placed on these herding dogs demanded many qualities. An intelligent dog who could counter a straying animal or control a group panicked into flight

An early German Shepherd.

would turn an impossible task for a shepherd into a simple routine.

With its extensive development of arable farming, Central Europe had no system of dividing hedges or dykes creating self-contained fields, such as was found in Britain. There were greater opportunities for sheep to stray from their allocated pasture land. To prevent such straying a herding dog would trot for hours round the flock to keep it within a designated area. A defensive ewe with her lamb, or a stubborn ram, would be countered by a competent dog with a measure of dominance without the aggression that would cause injury or panic within the flock. An excitable or sharp dog would cause a shepherd problems, rather than being a trusted helper.

The dogs favoured by shepherds were sensible and capable of thinking for themselves, but also of a calm and placid nature. The combination of these qualities was a result of nature, but was aided by selection. Trial and error in breeding from the most suitable males and females eventually produced dogs that suited shepherds' requirements. Looks were of no importance, although the structure of these dogs had to allow them to move easily for long periods, and also to take off at speed to counter some emergency. The dogs' coats were quite a mixture, some short, some with a wiry texture and others relatively long. The double coat – a thick woolly undercoat with a strong waterproof top coat to counter the variations in weather conditions – was very important.

The development of shepherding dogs in Germany by the end of the nineteenth century resulted in quite a variety of types. According to Joseph Schwabacher, the modern German Shepherd was developed by crossing the best dogs from the northern state of Württemberg with those of the central states of Frankonia and Thuringia.

The father of the breed was Captain Max von Stephanitz. His guiding hand from the end of the nineteenth century ensured the development of the German Shepherd Dog from a fragmentation of types into a single recognizable breed whose sole function was to be a working dog. The working objectives of the German Shepherd have been lost on many of today's breeders. However, the working ability developed throughout centuries of use and harnessed within one breed by von Stephanitz and his compatriots has endowed us with a very versatile domesticated animal.

This versatility has resulted in a dog which can be worked within many different activities but which, at the same time, is an ideal companion at home. Still used as a sheep-herding dog in his home country, the German Shepherd has proved to be very adaptable. Some have been selectively bred for their ability to guard, some as dedicated tracking dogs, others as guide dogs for the blind. Its versatility has resulted in the breed becoming first choice as working police dogs. Absolute control is required for basic obedience training. Independence and dedication are essential in scenting work, tracking and searching. Protection work makes great demands on courage. Yet the dog has to be answerable to his handler when the objective has been achieved. More than any other breed, the German Shepherd has proved itself capable of combining these special qualities.

CHAPTER 2

Temperament

Of all the important characteristics of the German Shepherd Dog, temperament is probably the most difficult to deal with. To use the questions put by Brian Wootton in *The German Shepherd Dog* (*see* Further Reading):

> What do we mean by temperament? How can we assess it? ... By temperament we mean the sum total of all those innate and acquired physical and mental qualities and capabilities that regulate, control and shape a dog's response to its environment. Temperament is a product of the interaction of environmental experiences and what a dog inherits from its ancestors, its genetic makeup.

Wootton also writes,

> The subject is notoriously complex since temperament is the sum total of many characteristics and behaviour patterns and its mode of inheritance is not properly understood.

Wootton has made it clear that temperament does not stand on its own and to some extent is dependent on all the lead characteristics discussed in Chapter 1. Temperament comes down to a dog's ability to harmonize with his environment – to accommodate environmental experiences. However, every puppy with an abil-

ity to accommodate life's experiences has an inherited level of that ability. That inherited level starts to change from the day it is born. In extreme cases there may only be one puppy born instead of a full litter – a lonesome pup. The dam may die as a result of the birth. The ensuing lack of companionship will affect the puppy's early weeks, and the manner in which a breeder handles such a situation can have an effect on a puppy's reaction to life. Throughout a dog's life circumstances will have their effect but inherited genetic characteristics will play a major role in a dog's ability to cope.

Puppies from the Nest

Males

Quest, my first German Shepherd, was born of good sound parents. He was one of a litter of nine. During his first eight weeks he was brought up in a quiet little country village with very few visitors. The breeder and his wife were the only company for the bitch and her litter. They had almost no one to come in and enjoy the presence of such a gorgeous litter of puppies. The dam was a pet at home, but she was continually on guard. Her bark and presence warned any unsolicited visitors. There was no doubt that

Eight weeks old, and Quest is gaining confidence.

such a defensive environmental experience could well affect a young puppy's outlook on life.

When we went to choose our puppy, it was clear that Quest and some of the others were not happy to meet visitors. It is interesting to look back and note that, even at that early stage, all the puppies did not have the same reactions. Genetic variations were already producing character differences. The owner of the sire was with us; he had the option of taking the pick of the litter. He was also going to advise us on our choice. Quest was recommended. This quiet puppy would suit a beginner like myself, with children at home.

During the first three days in his new home, with our two young daughters wanting to play with the puppy, Quest just did not want to know. The change was far too dramatic for this little fellow. I wondered if I had made a big mistake – but he was here to stay, and I felt responsible for ensuring that he would settle into our lifestyle.

I should now explain our previous interest in dogs. Before Quest there was Jed, our Labrador puppy. Unfortunately we lost him at the age of ten months through an infection. During his short life I had started taking Jed to training classes and I enjoyed this new activity. Not only did it suit me, but the family were able to participate too. They enjoyed coming along to the training sessions. We wanted to continue with this change of lifestyle.

I have said that Quest would have to settle into our way of life, but this was not strictly true. A dog coming into your life certainly changes it. Our leisure activities would now be built round Quest. He was to become the focal point in our lives.

After a short settling-in period of three days, Quest suddenly realized that his new home with the Cree family was not so bad. In fact it was to become very enjoyable. He accepted neighbours and friends without difficulty. Some neighbours, when they knew we were getting a German Shepherd (Alsatian at that time), were very worried because of the breed's reputation for being untrustworthy. I discovered early on that introducing puppies to neighbours is very important.

At the age of three months, Quest is enjoying a tug of war with young Joyce.

The neighbours' confidence and pleasure, along with your own demonstrated respect for their wishes, can help to ensure that early environmental experiences will be of a type which will give a puppy confidence. Quest, a little ball of fluff, mainly black with silver feet and a small patch of silver on his chest, was accepted straightaway. Nearly forty years on, he is still remembered with great warmth. These neighbours and friends still think Quest was 'something special'.

But those first few days in our home did concern me. At the time, we did not have transport of our own. It was a case of walking or public transport. During his inoculation period Quest could not be taken out. He was fourteen weeks old before he experienced the outside world. Today it is easier to take a puppy out in a car to visit friends or sometimes to an area which is dog-free. Puppies can now be exposed to the environment with much greater ease than in our early days. However, when Quest could be taken out he became accustomed to pub-

lic transport very quickly. He was taken into town on the bus every Saturday morning and walked through the busy streets. A short spell in this crowded area worked wonders.

Further stories of Quest will show that his inbred temperament was sound, but had he remained with the breeder in a quiet secluded atmosphere, he could well have grown into an adult dog with many uncertainties.

Callum was completely different. He was born a little 'toughy' and finished up with a number of nicknames. At home, he became known as the original German barge dog. He would barge here, there and everywhere. No ornament was safe unless it was high up, or on a fixed or solid piece of furniture. Buying Callum was the start of another chapter in our lives.

Quest was getting on in years and Tanya, our first bitch, had taken an early retirement from competitive work. I was looking for a new puppy. Tanya's litter-sister, Honey, had been mated to a stud-dog I had already used on Tanya herself

Callum would tackle anything.

and I had liked the results. We went to see Honey's puppies when they were three weeks old. They were in a barn, where bales of straw created a compound for the puppies. As we looked into this compound, one little sable pup, a deceptive-looking 'butter-ball', looked at us, stood four-square, and gave a defiant little bark. He turned away and ignored us. Having the choice of this litter, I said to the breeder, 'That's the one for me.' Callum was booked – and was going to be quite a challenge.

At eight weeks old Callum was brought to his new home and settled in straight away. There were two other German Shepherds at home. Their presence would help, but I am sure he would have settled without any other canine company. His first sign of dominance showed within a few days. He had a tug-of-war with a worm which was determined to disappear into the lawn. Callum latched on one end, with the other end of the worm well into the ground. It was only my intervention which allowed the worm to make its way underground and away from this little horror. Everything about

Callum told us that arrogance should be his middle name, but at the age of four to five months doubts would come into his mind. Three instances gave us cause to think again.

We took him to the training club for the first time, just as an introduction to the atmosphere. I was one of the trainers and Callum could just sit and watch. We opened the door of the hall to go in, but the noise of people talking and dogs barking hit Callum. He dug his heels in. 'I'm not going in there,' was his attitude. 'Oh yes you are son,' was mine. I gave a tug on the lead and we were in. A couple of steps into the doorway, an Afghan with its owner was coming out. It snapped at Callum, without a thought that this little fellow might dare to retaliate. Only the fact that I was on the other end of the lead prevented contact. Callum would stand no nonsense from a dog that was disrespectful towards him.

We were out for a walk along the river bank, the whole family, dogs and the girls, now teenagers. There was a very narrow bridge over the river, which we had crossed quite often. The bridge was a single piece of wood about fifteen inches (40cm) wide and thirty feet (10m) long, with side-rails for support. This was Callum's first venture across a bridge. The dogs, Irene and the girls were all across, but Callum refused to move. Looking down at the water, petrified and shaking, he was thinking 'That's not for me.' With lead attached, I got down on my hands and knees to crawl backwards across the bridge, coaxing Callum to follow. He moved forward slowly, one short step at a time before thinking about the next one. Eventually we got across, and had some fun in the field before returning to cross the bridge again. Dogs first – up the steps and across the bridge, with Callum running behind them as if he had been doing this all of his short life.

Further along the river bank there was a lock. One day, Callum stopped as we reached it and looked at a mooring bollard. He backed off and would not pass it. We all passed the bollard but Callum would not. What sort of evil this conjured in his mind we did not know. Fear had raised an uncertainty. I went over and leaned on the bollard, called the family to come over and we started to have fun with the other dogs. This was too much for Callum: his fear was being ignored and they were having fun. Slowly he came to us, sniffed the bollard, then said to himself, 'Silly me!' The bollard was no longer a problem.

Callum quickly grew out of these uncertainties. It was a very short phase in his life, probably about two or three weeks. Uncertainties of this kind never surfaced with Quest after his first few days in our home. Everything about Callum told us he was going to be a hard dog. He was a 'smine' ('It's mine') dog. Everything belonged to him.

In using my own dogs Quest and Callum as examples, I have first-hand knowledge of the differences in their genetic make-up, and of the inherited characteristics that determined their temperaments. Quest was of a softer nature and Callum very much harder. The breeding and era of both dogs differed. Quest was principally English-type breeding of the 1950s, whereas Callum's sire was a German import who would have been described in his home country as having plenty of temperament, spirit and energy. Both dogs, in maturity, were of completely different types regarding the various characteristics that determine temperament. Although they lived in similar environments and had one master, they required different approaches to training and had different ways of coping with life. Both made equally good pets at home and both achieved great success in Working Trials, qualifying Police Dog Excellent.

Females

I have made comparisons between two of the male dogs that came in to our home at the 'right age' – eight weeks old. It now seems appropriate to make a comparison between two of our bitches under similar conditions. (It must be said that conditions are never identical. Quest was our only companion in his youth. Callum had Quest and Tanya as canine companions who could help him settle in, but Callum was the type of dog who would not require such help.)

The two bitches to be compared are Tanya and Kerry. Tanya was introduced when Quest was approaching three years of age. Kerry joined Quest and Tanya about five years later.

Tanya was our first bitch. She arrived at Edinburgh Airport from Ireland. Irene was there to meet her late one Friday afternoon. Her journey home was by coach into Edinburgh, train to Dundee, then a bus trip home to Broughty Ferry. This was quite a journey for an eight-week-old who had already made a car journey and then a flight across the Irish Sea. However, Tanya took it in her stride, and settled in with a good meal, giving the impression that she was thinking, 'If this is my new home, what next?'

That first night she settled into her new bed in the kitchen. Not a sound. She was probably tired after her hectic journey. In the morning we heard noises when we woke up, but could not understand the cause. Into the kitchen we went to see what Tanya had been up to. The floor was littered with Brussels sprouts and potatoes. She was having a whale of a time. First lesson: keep things secure at night.

Unfortunately, I had no time to give Tanya during this first weekend. A family bereavement preoccupied me, then I was back at work on the Monday; so it was the following weekend before I could give her any time. This first week with the Cree family proved to be very significant to Tanya's outlook throughout her life.

Quest was very much the family dog but, because of the time I devoted to training and competing with him, I did have the edge in that Quest saw me primarily as pack leader. Tanya, on the other hand, because of her first week, was now Irene's dog. She had brought her home from the airport, and looked after her needs for a whole week. As time went on I could train her, work her and feed her, but during that first week I lost her. Irene was probably accepted as her

surrogate mother during those first few hours of travelling home. I had no problems with Tanya. She was not defiant. She was just Irene's dog. The lesson I learned from Tanya was the importance of those first few hours and days if you want to train a dog for competition work. After that, I arranged to have the first few days free to welcome any other puppy into our home.

Tanya had a great deal of spirit and character – at times too much, or so it seemed. She loved to play with the children, but if the girls got too excited she would nip their bottoms. Lessons were there to be learned before the situation got out of hand. As a young puppy Tanya did launch herself at the grocer when he was making a delivery. Fortunately no damage was done and he was an understanding friend. Such an opportunity was never given again until Tanya had learned that not all strangers to the door were unwelcome. Her sharpness did rear its head again when I started training with Quest for criminal work in preparation for the Police Dog Stakes in Working Trials. If Tanya was present, she had a natural instinct to get involved, and took some controlling. It was safer to keep her out of the way during these training sessions.

Kerry could not have been more different from Tanya. She was my mistake, an impulse decision. It would not be fair to blame her for her problems in life.

Quest had been mated to a bitch of show breeding with no real working qualities in her pedigree. She was a nice bitch, a pleasant one to have about the house. I had seen her often enough in her own surroundings and at the training club. She was nice, but her character had little impact on me. I had no intention of taking a puppy, although I could have had the pick of the litter in lieu of a stud fee.

Most of the puppies were sold and two were left – a dog and a bitch. The breeder had already planned to have a short holiday. To let her have her holiday we took the two eight-week-old puppies and would hope to have them sold by the time the breeder came home. The dog puppy was sold but the bitch was still with us when the breeder returned. This puppy was an affectionate little thing and was quite attached to me; I had known her since she could open her eyes. We decided to take her instead of a stud fee. This was Kerry.

Kerry had already decided that I was God's gift to a little puppy. This proved to be our undoing. I had time to give her attention in the evenings, and we both enjoyed the little stints of basic training. The other dogs were not neglected and were quite happy to accept their new companion. With her nature, Kerry was no threat to the established pecking order, and was quite content to accept Quest and Tanya in their leading roles.

Life changed for me. I was promoted to Head Office in London. As we lived in Bishop's Stortford at the time, my travelling and extended hours of work left very little time or energy for anything, except at weekends. All three dogs required their daily exercise. The morning walk before work did me no harm. Irene would take them out during the day. There was little time for more than a walk in the evenings.

Kerry had really taken to me. She became very broody during the day whilst I was at work. She would get on to my armchair and stay there most of the day. She was the only dog to be given that privilege. Thinking back, this privilege may not have been wise. It may have con-

tributed to her broodiness. I had created a situation and Kerry could not handle it. Another lesson to be learned. We discussed the situation and thought of rehoming her; but what home would suit her? Where would she get the kind of attention she deserved and required? We discussed this – but always backed away from a decision. We had never parted with an adult dog before, only puppies from the nest. When a puppy came into our home it was for life. Then, when Kerry about about two years of age, something happened which made it clear that action had to be taken.

Tanya had been mated and produced a litter of four puppies. Kerry was always subservient to Tanya and she loved these puppies. I sometimes wonder if there was some prehistoric pack instinct which caused Kerry to feel protective over Tanya as well as the puppies.

One evening while I was away, Irene and our daughter Joyce took Tanya for her first walk after she had finished nursing her puppies. Kerry was with them. They met a friend of Joyce's in uniform, on her way to a Guide meeting. While chatting, the friend bent down to pat Tanya, saying, 'Aren't you a clever Mum with four babies to look after?' At that, Kerry sprang forward and nipped her on the arm. It was only a bruise, but her blouse was torn. This came out of the blue. Kerry had never shown any indication of aggression to human or dog in the past, one bite could lead to another. We could only conclude that she felt the need to protect the mother of those pups at home. When I returned home that evening I was shattered to hear the story. Irene had already been round to see the family, who accepted our apologies. This event renewed our thoughts of a home for

Kerry that would give her greater satisfaction. We felt responsible for her attitude to life.

The following day she was entered in an Obedience competition that was to be judged by the trainers from Debden which, at that time, was the dog training centre for the Royal Air Force. Kerry gained 99 marks out of 100 and finished second after a run-off for first place. I was very friendly with the trainers at Debden and asked Bob Bruce, the assistant head trainer, whether he thought there might be a place for Kerry in the R.A.F. Bob was taken completely by surprise. 'You wouldn't part with her, would you?' I told him the whole story, then continued, 'She would be no use for normal guard duties, and I don't think she could go to any handler. Would you be interested in having her for your demonstration team?'

Arrangements were made, and Irene and I took her to Debden. We met the head trainer and the officer commanding the base, and were open and honest about the circumstances. I also gave them more details of her abilities. In training, and in life in general, it had become apparent that Kerry had a tremendous desire to jump and climb. Working Trials agility had come very easily to her. The six-foot scale-jump, three-foot clear and nine-foot long jumps were just fun. She would jump over anything when asked, and with great pleasure. She would even confidently climb up a part-fallen tree that was lying at an angle of 45 degrees, then turn round and come down again.

The R.A.F. were interested, especially when they saw what she could do. I made it clear that Kerry needed to be given plenty of work and attention, with no time to brood, then rest in a tired state of mind. It was agreed that if she failed to make the grade, and was rejected at any time, we would take her back. Kerry was accepted, and was handed to a sergeant whose older dog was retiring. She went into serious training for the demonstration team.

Months later we went to see Kerry at the Royal Tournament in London. She performed the tightrope walk then carried the flaming dumb-bell – the highlight of the demonstration. We were so proud of her, and of our own decision to let her go. We were also very grateful to the R.A.F. and to her handler for giving young Kerry a new life. She received an early discharge to stay with her handler when he retired, and enjoyed the rest of her life with him.

There is no doubt that any delay in transferring a puppy into its new environment can cause its own problems. The complexities of genetics control a dog's character and temperament at the start of his life. The inclusion of environmental factors helps to determine the pleasures he gives and receives. To take a puppy straight from the nest at about eight weeks of age is ideal for shaping its future. The breeder has played his part. The inherited temperament was his responsibility.

One particular instance of how problems could have occured through delayed transfer was little Isla. She was booked for ourselves along with Chisum, her brother, for our daughter Joyce. As it turned out I was due to judge at Working Trials and we would be away from home for a short period. The puppies would be ten weeks old when it would be convenient to collect them. The breeder agreed to keep them for the extra two weeks. These puppies were from parents of

The tightrope walk.

superb temperament and character. Problems were the last thing we expected.

When the puppies were just coming up to eight weeks old, the breeder phoned me. 'Your little bitch is starting to go back into her shell. I strongly advise you to come down for her. Get her into a fresh environment.' This breeder was experienced and thoughtful, and knew what he was talking about. His advice made us make the 560-mile (900km) round trip to bring both puppies home at eight weeks.

Joyce looked after both puppies while we were away. I doubt if she has forgiven us for leaving her with two little troublemakers together. Two puppies can more than double the problems of one.

It turned out that both puppies had tremendous character, but we will never know if an extra two weeks in the nest would have made a difference to that. A considerate breeder did not want to take the risk.

Older Puppies

There are many reasons why older puppies are offered for sale. There are also many reasons why people wish to buy puppies that have passed through the earlier stages of development.

Breeders run puppies on for showing, only to discover that they do not come up to the winning standard. These puppies generally come on to the market at about eight to ten months old, when the breeder decides to trade them in for cash. Some breeders seem to have an endless breeding programme, with selected puppies from each litter being run on until they become adults.

Some may do very well in the show ring as puppies until maturity highlights faults that were not apparent in the youngsters. Economics then dictates that a kennel clearance sale is required to reduce costs and to enhance the bank balance. More dogs on the market. Dogs with little or no experience of life outside the kennel or the show ring are released with a price tag. This happens with all breeds of dog. German Shepherds are no exception. These dogs may or may not have been born with a good inherited temperament but most have not been environmentally equipped for life in the community.

There are also dogs who have left the nest at the right age, but who go into homes that prove to be unsuitable in one way or another. These youngsters are then sold, with excuses for having to part with them. Mainly they are just excuses.

Young dogs may come from a rescue centre. Experience of the problems encountered by those who have acquired such dogs has told me that the real reason for the dogs being in these centres is not generally given, and may not even be known by the rescue centre organizers. There is nothing wrong with taking on an older puppy or young adult, provided you appreciate that some hidden reason may have resulted in the animal becoming available.

Why do people look for older puppies or young adults instead of a puppy from the nest? Again there are various reasons. More often than not, these owners do not wish to be involved with puppy training from the earliest stages. It can be too much bother for some people, but normally they take on larger problems with the purchase of an older dog. Some people find it difficult to wait for a new puppy to become available when an old faithful has died and left a void in the home. There are occasions when a prospective buyer visits various kennels looking for a puppy from the nest, and is persuaded by the breeder to take on an older one that just happened to be available. Kennel temperament can be very misleading. A

youngster that seems to be free and easy on his own home ground can turn out to be frightened of his own shadow when faced with the outside world. Sound inherited temperament can be ruined by extended kennel life.

Three situations that are worthy of comment have come to mind. Two of them concern my own dogs, but the third is much more important. This involved an unsuspecting couple who, when looking for a puppy from the nest, were persuaded by the breeder to take on an eight-month-old puppy she just happened to have available. I shall call this young dog Kate. The husband wanted to train the puppy for Working Trials, and the breeder persuaded him that Kate was just right for the purpose, and could start training without delay. Her previous history was not discussed with the trusting couple.

Kate had been sold at the age of eight weeks to a family who had never owned a dog before. Their twelve-year-old daughter wanted a German Shepherd and kept on and on about getting one. The parents were quite sensible about it. They realized that if they took on a puppy it would be a family responsibility, not just that of their daughter, so it was agreed that everyone would take a share in attending to Kate's needs. Dad would take the puppy for her morning walk before he went to work. Mum, at home all day, would attend to Kate's daytime needs, puppy training, feeding and exercising. The daughter would give Kate her early evening walk, and attending to the needs of nature during the evening would be shared. Too often, Kate's needs clashed with the girl's television viewing.

Kate was about six months old when she started cringing in the corner and

The cringing pose assumed by Kate when the little girl came near.

growling at the daughter when she went near the puppy. This puzzled the parents who contacted a behaviourist/dog trainer by telephone for advice. Subsequent questioning revealed that sometimes when Kate had to be taken out for a walk or a call of nature and there was a good programme on the television, the daughter did not want to go out but was told, 'Come on, you promised to take your turn at looking after Kate. Be fair to the puppy. Take her out now'.

It transpired that when the door closed behind Kate and the daughter, the puppy would give a yelp. Although the girl always had an explanation – 'she caught her tail in the door' or 'she accidentally stood on her paw' – it was obvious that this unpleasant child took her frustration out on Kate in some form of physical abuse,

probably a spiteful kick. The behaviourist had unearthed the cause of the problem but heard no more from the parents. A few weeks later he contacted them to see if the situation had been resolved. He was informed that the daughter and Kate were just not compatible, and that the breeder had taken Kate back.

Some months later a couple brought a nice-looking German Shepherd bitch to the behaviourist's training class for basic training. The bitch's name was Kate, and she was very nervous. The couple had just bought her from a local breeding kennel. This was the same Kate that had been abused by an inconsiderate and selfish child.

Kate's eyes told their own story, darting and watching every movement with an obvious fear of everything round her. She had been taken lovingly from the kennel at eight weeks, and then abused for no good reason. She had been returned to the kennels and her litter-mates had all gone. She was alone. When she needed comfort, particularly from human beings, it was not there. Kate went further back into her shell, with no trust for the outside world.

Kate's new owners now had a problem. She was distrustful of everything except her new owners, who became the anchor she was looking for. Outside the home or with visitors she was a bag of nerves and ready to give a defensive nip at any unsuspecting person who came along. The inevitable happened: she bit an unsuspecting acquaintance before she could be stopped. Kate was put to sleep.

Who was to blame? One unpleasant child was certainly an important factor. The breeder who resold a dog which had a known major problem must bear a great responsibility, especially when the new owners were kept in the dark about the problem.

Jeza came into our home when she was about six months old. She was a pretty little bitch, and she took my eye while she was at the breeding kennels, but her background was not a happy one. I was taking club training sessions on the breeder's grounds and spending a bit of time at the kennels. I was getting to know a number of the breeder's own German Shepherds quite well.

One day, I happened to be at the kennels when a couple came to look at a litter of puppies. They arrived in a Rolls-Royce and it was apparent that the price of a puppy would not break the bank. They wanted two puppies to take home, a dog and a bitch. The couple would be living in the UK for the next few months before returning to their permanent

home overseas. The puppies were eight weeks old and the couple had no problems in choosing two lively little youngsters. It was a nice litter, whose breeding should have resulted in good outgoing temperaments.

The next I knew of the two puppies was on a visit to the kennels three months later. They had been returned to the breeder. The story as relayed was one of health problems. I cannot recall the list, but elbow-joint problems were claimed to have been the principal reason for these two youngsters being discarded. After a few weeks at home with the Rolls-Royce owners, the puppies were dumped on a vet who looked after them for a few more weeks. The complaints were passed on to the breeder, who promptly picked the puppies up from the vet's surgery and brought them back to the kennels.

The breeder took both puppies, and another she was keeping, to the veterinary college for a comprehensive examination to determine if these problems existed and, if so, whether they were inherited. All three puppies received a clean bill of health. Perhaps the couple who bought the two puppies had found that they could not cope with youngsters so full of life and mischief. Two fun-loving and unpredictable puppies together create much more trouble than one. Although I do not know the outcome of the dispute between the breeder and the original purchasers, I learnt that the puppies were back on the market.

The unsettled time and the lack of affection they had experienced during those formative weeks did not constitute the ideal conditions for the future character of any puppy. However, with full knowledge of her background, we bought the bitch puppy. We did not know her

Jeza with young Caro (the dark sable), posing with the author for a photo call in 1976. (Photo. Marc Henrie.)

name, so she started her new life with us as Jeza. Her character and temperament seemed to have survived the earlier disruption. Her parentage was one of successful show stock, with no working qualities in her breeding.

From all this it could be inferred that training Jeza would prove to be a challenge. Her biggest handicap was her inability to play with me, or with toys. I am sure this was not an inherited deficiency but rather the result of the disadvantage that she had experienced so early in her life. Her brother had been her play companion, and as a result she was dog-orientated at that stage of her life. It took some time to create a change. In my training classes I have often come across dogs of all breeds who do not know how to play. Their owners have never played with them, and have turned them into dull, uninteresting dogs, ruining their natural zest for life.

In due course, Jeza did learn the joys of living, especially when her hidden qualities were discovered. Her interest in birds in flight encouraged her to retrieve discs and the like. Salmon leaping in the river would prompt her to jump in to try and find them. She never caught one, but it was a real joy to see the pleasure she got from the activity.

The look in Ceilidh's eyes warns us that she has a short fuse.

Jeza never gave us an ounce of trouble. She was a lovable pet, but lacked the sparkle expected from the breed. Did these first few months create this condition? I do not know, but I do suspect that the early part of her life did her no favours. A dog from more extrovert breeding may well have been able to handle the situation better.

Caro had a different beginning to his life. He was fifteen weeks old when we brought him home from the breeder. We had met his sire some time earlier at a GSD League Rally. He had tremendous character and temperament. He was a real fun dog, full of spirit and vitality, but sensible.

I was making tentative enquiries about matings by a few stud-dogs of my choice, in preparation to selecting a new companion for Jeza. A litter by Caro's sire had just arrived on the scene, but I was not quite ready to take a puppy. It was a dilemma because this litter interested me very much. The puppies were of top-class show breeding with excellent working potential. I came to an arrangement with the breeder that she would keep a suitable puppy until I was ready to take him at the age of fifteen weeks. The puppy would be inoculated and, most important, he would be socialized so that I would not have a puppy at that age raw from the kennel. The manner in which Caro settled in when we brought him home made it clear that the breeder had done an excellent job.

There is always a tendency to compare one of your dogs with another. We always

Ceilidh in a very misleading pose.

looked on Quest as a 'canine gentleman' with Callum as the 'tough guy'. Caro's outlook on life was about midway between the two. Except for travel-sickness as a puppy, he was without hang-ups. Those extra few weeks with his breeder, receiving the proper attention and being socialized, ensured that he came to us with an active and receptive mind.

Puppies with a 'Short Fuse'

A puppy that is genetically endowed with a short fuse is one thing, but when that fuse is of the fast-burning variety then a loss of temper can be as vigorous and unpredictable as an erupting volcano. Some German Shepherd puppies are so laid back that nothing will cause them to lose their tempers. Others do not seem to require an excuse. Ceilidh and Strachan were two such puppies.

When Ceilidh arrived in our home at the age of eight weeks, she trotted through to the lounge and spotted a teddy bear which Irene had knitted as a welcoming toy. Ceilidh's immediate reaction was to grab the teddy, shake the living daylights out of it, drop it, turn and walk away with the attitude, 'I am the Alpha bitch in this house. Everything submits to me'. The pecking order had been established. That was the first of many shakings poor teddy had to endure. It seemed that when Ceilidh felt she was being dominated by Irene or myself the pecking order was reinforced, with teddy at the bottom of the pile.

Excitability was like putting a match to a fuse. I have always enjoyed a rough and tumble on the floor with my puppies. With Ceilidh it would be in earnest. Her needle-sharp puppy teeth left their mark. Irene never got down to play with Ceilidh, but her hands were covered with puncture marks.

My fun and games with Ceilidh were turned into training sessions, one of temper control. Create a measure of excitability, then apply firm control with a follow-up of gentle praise. It was going to take time, but this little wild one had to be tamed without overwhelming the natural spirit and vitality of such a vivacious creature.

Ceilidh's wickedness became most evident to our vet. It was time for a check-up, inoculation and worming. She was ten weeks old and had accepted handling from the vet with no problem, until the vet decided to pop a large worming tablet down her throat. Ceilidh was very firmly held, mouth prised open and the tablet expertly put well down so that she could not spit it out. The look in her eyes told it all. The ignited fuse had caused a full detonation. Her eyes were alight with an anger and hatred I had never seen before in an animal. The vet looked at me with a knowing smile, 'You're going to have a problem with this one.' She was right. Ceilidh would never have survived with owners who lacked the experience to handle such a dominant and disruptive youngster.

By the time Ceilidh was six months old she had settled. Her first season also contributed to a calmer and more mature attitude to life. Now, in middle life, she is as laid back and as sensible as the best. A real pleasure to live with.

Strachan in a temper was quite different: his reaction was like that of a volcano. When in a passive mood he was a joyful, fun-loving youngster, but in full eruption he showed the most violent aggression I have ever known in a puppy of any breed.

A Born Pack Leader

I met Strachan for the first time when he was eleven weeks old. He belonged to our elder daughter, Frances, who lived some 450 miles away from us. We were spending a long weekend break with the family. Strachan was from a German sire with very strong characteristics, and it seemed that he had inherited most of his genes from that source. Frances bought him at the age of nine weeks. He was a bundle of energy and vitality, but a build-up of excitement could take him over the top. The look in his eyes told its own story. His bites were not little puppy nips but clearly demonstrated his intent: aggressive domination. Frances and her husband, Colin, were fully aware of the situation and were concerned about countering the activities of this little monster; they called him the puppy from hell.

One of the problems manifested itself in the puppy's relationship with Elaine, our fourteen-year-old granddaughter. She just loved to play with puppies. She had been brought up with German Shepherds, right from the puppy stage. However, with Strachan, the excitement generated by such fun and games usually ended in tears when his reactions got out of hand. He was establishing his pecking order. I saw this for myself during our short visit. Hearing a noise from the sitting room, I opened the door to a horrifying scene. Elaine, a big girl for her age, was on the settee but was cringing and crouched, sobbing, as little Strachan snarled and tried to get at her. He meant business. The pair of them had been playing, and things had got out of hand.

This situation could not be tolerated. If a child cannot play with a young puppy without such a vicious response, something has to be done. There was no doubt that Strachan's attitude at that moment was one of domination. He was sorting out the pecking order in the only way he knew. I dived into the room, caught him by the scruff of the neck, turned him onto his back, and held him there to submit. He had to learn to control himself, and total submission was the only way. I held him there for what seemed like an eternity. He struggled, he shook his head, he kicked his feet, trying everything to get free. He was determined not to submit; I was equally determined that he would. This was a contest of wills. To let him win now was a short road to disaster. Eventually, he gave in.

A family conference was called to discuss how to handle Strachan and Elaine. Unfortunately, she could no longer play with the puppy. She was frightened of him and would now keep clear of him until he had developed some self-control and greater respect for every member of the family. The submission routine was to be applied any time Strachan thought of dominating a situation, but it took years for Elaine to accept his presence without fear or distrust.

Strachan was born to be a pack leader. Any animal seeking dominance with such aggression would create problems in a wild pack. He may not reach maturity within the social structure. He might be driven out by older and higher-ranking males; but if he survived, he would make a very effective pack leader. A real Alpha male.

As Strachan developed it became obvious that he had been born with very strong working qualities. Frances trained him for Working Trials. He was manageable when he was not pushed into doing something he did not want to do, an assessment that Frances summed up with

the comment, 'Strachan pleases me when it pleases him to please me.' Any objection would bring his stubborn dominance to the surface again. Frances coped until there was a change in circumstances.

Colin, Frances' husband, was a police dog-handler. Aran, his working dog, was coming to the end of his operational life. He and Strachan got on well together. Aran, although he served Colin very well, was a 'canine gentleman' like Quest. Strachan did not consider him a challenge to his Alpha status. Colin was now looking for a replacement. Various gift dogs were taken in for testing and assessment.

With hindsight, it was obvious that to bring another male dog into the home would upset Strachan. There was no direct contact between these gift dogs and Strachan, but their presence caused his dominance to reappear. He was making life very difficult for Frances, and she would phone me for help and advice. Strachan was becoming unpredictable, and she could no longer handle the situation. Strachan was now fully mature, over two years of age. He was a good competition worker, and had qualified C.D.Ex. and U.D.Ex. His tracking was excellent, he was a good searching dog, and his agility and control work were also good. He had all the makings of a good police dog. I asked whether the police could take him at that age, and have Colin handle him. This would be the ideal solution, and would suit Colin. Strachan was accepted by the police and completed his training for operational duties to create a new working partnership.

Strachan happily accepted his new role. When he walked out of Frances's life, he became Colin's dog. He had never bonded with Frances, never indicated any affection, except for a short spell when he was ill. Frances had done everything for Strachan. She fed him, walked him and worked him, but he gave nothing in return. Colin had taken a back seat until he took over the dog. When Colin took him, Frances felt as if the dog had died. A huge burden had been taken from her shoulders. For the next year Strachan was never in the house, and he could not have cared less: he had a job of work to do, he had his own kennel, and he had Colin. He was a man's dog, and it seemed that in his mind Frances had ceased to exist.

There were occasions when Strachan's strength of will showed through, but Colin had the ability and dominance to master it. Strachan always knew that Colin would win, but he kept challenging.

Training for 'Send away' was one example when he would leave Colin, then show a reluctance to do any more. With the 'Search' exercise he would willingly hunt for the articles, but then they were his. He was extremely possessive. The 'Send away' was always a weakness in the armoury of Strachan's performances.

As the years rolled by, Strachan began to mellow. He retired from the police along with Colin and became a pet dog, with spells in the house. He now has the ability to show affection to the family. Colin also has a young German Shepherd called Jasper, an easy-going dog without any vices. He has been accepted by Strachan without any signs of aggression, even when they are play-fighting. Perhaps Jasper is no challenge and Strachan is content to enjoy some peace in his retirement.

CHAPTER 3

Loyalty

Loyalty is a form of emotional commitment. To understand and recognize it generates an attitude of responsibility. To understand loyalty between dog and man requires a very wide interpretation of the subject. As a starting point, it may be appropriate to consider emotional commitment between human beings. It has often been said that the emotions of human beings cannot be applied to the thinking or emotional reactions of dogs and I accept that theory in principle. But we can learn about canine loyalty by examining human commitment and obligations.

Emotional commitment controls our lives, but we all have our own interpretations of what it means, to ourselves and to others. There are degrees of loyalty. Any individual could consider his or her loyalties or obligations and place them in order of commitment. Examples might be: spouse, close family or more distant relations, employer or employees, neighbours or social friends, bank managers, sporting partners, sport or social clubs. The list could be very long. Some of these categories will carry extremely strong emotional obligations while others receive a very low status of obligation or commitment.

One person may well have a greater commitment to his golf club than to his wife. A wealthy but ageing mother-in-law may receive a higher degree of emotional commitment than an employer. Self-preservation may help to dictate someone's emotional priorities. This reminds me of the interpretation of canine logic that I quoted earlier: 'A dog will always do what he considers to be in his best interest at that particular moment in time.' This can easily be interpreted in human terms.

It may be a rather cynical point of view, but I believe that a German Shepherd has a greater understanding of moral obligations and commitment than many members of the human race.

The questions to be considered are:

1. What is loyalty?
2. Loyalty to whom or what?
3. What are the constituents of loyalty?

What is Loyalty?

As already discussed, loyalty is an emotional commitment or obligation. But how does it show itself?

Fidelity

This can be expressed as being faithful and honest. Such a commitment may be the expectation between a husband and wife. This can also be classified as a sexual commitment. Canine fidelity with man is purely a commitment of companionship. A special relationship where the

Quest in training, and demonstrating the will to serve.

the relationship between a working German Shepherd and his handler. Social and leisure activities also highlight the importance of this kind of commitment.

Obedience and Desire to Conform

This may appear to come from a strict, uncompromising regime and this cannot be denied. This kind of loyalty implies an understanding that there is a purpose behind laws and rules. Company rules, those of social clubs, and those within the family community create the obligation to conform. A German Shepherd will also appreciate, although may not understand in human terms, that obedience and desire to conform create an enjoyable environment which encourages a reaction of loyalty.

Respect

This has to be earned. German Shepherds can be more discriminating than people in interpreting the true measure of respect. I think that man probably has much more to learn in creating a respectful relationship with his canine companion that does the dog.

master is an anchor – the most important enduring and caring union between man and dog.

Devotion and Allegiance

This carries a strength of commitment within a close family or social circle including the dog, who understands his rightful place within that environment. This devotion and allegiance carry an obligation from each member of that close circle.

Obligation and Will to Serve

This may seem more appropriate to the employer–employee relationship, but it can also be recognized in the canine world, in

Loyalty to Whom or What?

As an emotional obligation, loyalty is a necessity in life, and covers a very wide field.

Loyalty Between People

Harmony within a community would be non-existent without loyalty. It embraces obligations towards others, a person's principles and the causes he believes in.

Caro and Isla enjoying a session at the beach without giving reason to fear that they will abuse their freedom.

Loyalty Between German Shepherd and Man

Initially we think of a German Shepherd's loyalty as his commitment to his master, to the family he lives with, or to close friends. Some German Shepherds find it easy to transfer that commitment to people they have never met before, provided those people show a sufficient degree of feeling towards the dog to achieve a temporary attachment. A friendship can then develop and become more permanent, with commitment or obligation on both sides.

It may be thought that a German Shepherd is a 'one-man dog', that he will not transfer his commitment easily. A great many do not, but a dog's survival instinct can induce a transfer of commitment if he feels abandoned or abused. How does a German Shepherd puppy feel when he is taken from the nest, and leaves his mother and litter-mates for a new home? Even the best of ownership transfers can be very stressful. Remember Quest and his first days of uncertainty until he realized that his new home gave him warmth, shelter, feeding and affection – the ingredients necessary to establish a new and lasting commitment.

When an older German Shepherd, with much more experience of life, suddenly discovers that his surroundings have changed and his master or mistress is new, he is likely to undergo a period of uncertainty before making any type of commitment to his new environment. If the dog has been taken from an uncaring home without love and affection, with cruelty as the emotional background, the change to a caring and affectionate home where his requirements are understood and appreciated should soon turn initial suspicion and uncertainty into enduring gratitude. A possible danger

The best of friends: Caro and Sharon, who worked together on a BBC television series, 'The Mad Death' (see Chapter 10).

here is that the emotional commitment and obligation from the dog may become overpowering. If not properly handled, or if the damage is irreparable, this can result in a form of loyalty which may distort the dog's characteristics, creating an unfavourable imbalance of temperament.

The case of Kate, described in Chapter 2, is an extreme, but not uncommon, example. A youngster, having been abused, suffered an unsettled period before finding a happy home, and finally gave total loyalty and commitment to her saviours. Her defensive mechanism became unbalanced. She was suspicious of any possible interference in her relationship with her new master and mistress. Attack was her only means of defence, so she was classed as an unpredictable and dangerous dog. Result: a one-way trip to the vet.

Some German Shepherds, although they retain their balance of characteristics, can

A mother and son relationship that created a tremendous bond.

find change to be very difficult. Rod was one such dog. He was bought at the age of eight weeks by David and Mary as a replacement for a dear departed canine friend. David would train this youngster for Obedience competitions. His old dog had been reasonably successful but never hit the high spots. The principal problem was put down to split loyalty. The old boy would work for David, but Mary's presence (and, on occasions, her absence) prevented 100 per cent attention at the critical times in competition. David was going to make sure Rod would be his dog, with loyalty and commitment to him alone.

The puppy slept at his feet in the evening. When David got out of his chair to go to the kitchen or the loo, Rod was given every encouragement to follow him. When he was old enough David took him

to work with him. At lunchtime he trained Rod in the car park. The dog spent his days either in the car or with David in the office. He was never left with Mary unless there was no alternative.

Rod's training continued. He responded well, although he was a late developer. German Shepherds, when compared with Border Collies, take time to mature. Patience was required and was applied. Although he was not winning events he was usually well placed. His performances were dependable and very satisfying.

When Rod was about four years of age, David left Mary. He had found a new love in his life – someone who was very uncertain about the dog. Rod had turned out to be a large, handsome but harmless German Shepherd and was now being left with Mary. David did take him to his new home at some time during weekends to try and have his new love accept Rod as one of their family. It did not work out. Rod became very unsettled: which home was which?

When with Mary, Rod sat at the window looking and waiting for his master. Eventually David lost all interest in his dog. The breakdown of the marriage was complete. Rod was discarded like a broken toy. It is commonly said in competition circles that to leave your wife is one thing, but to desert your dog is unforgivable. Rod was born to be a man's dog. Without David, he turned to Mary for the affection she was happy to give him. She became the new anchor in his life. He became committed. Loyalty was transferred to someone who really cared for him.

In due course Mary met Dick, a water bailiff living on a large estate. He protected the fishing rights along the river. Dick's visits resulted in a new relationship for Rod. He liked this man of authority who had respect for the requirements of a dog. Authority and respect with understanding and affection was music to Rod's ears. Working on an estate, Dick was accustomed to the various gun-dog breeds. This German Shepherd was something different. The intelligence, the alertness and the look of confidence which had returned to Rod's outlook was helping to create a real bond. A partnership was in the making.

Mary moved in with Dick. Rod was his constant companion during his duties on the estate. He became the 'ears' at night, out on patrol for poachers. His sense of smell brought out his natural tracking instinct to follow and locate a hidden poacher. He had found a new 'dad', a new way of life, with loyalty which was based on respect, trust and good companionship. A commitment from both parties.

Mary had not lost Rod, but now felt her family was complete.

Loyalty between German Shepherds

This is a most natural form of loyalty. Two animals of their own kind: what better than a male German Shepherd with a bitch for company? Such loyalty is common, but the introduction of a third dog can result in a changed relationship. Male and female together will form a strong bond of commitment. A third means two of the same sex, resulting in possible friction. This can cause an atmosphere of conflict rather than family unity. Pecking order can be more difficult to resolve.

As a consultant I have found that owners who buy or keep litter-brothers or -sisters as pets at home are most likely to have problems. As the youngsters go through adolescence and into maturity, the consolidation of character can create two animals with similar aspirations of Alpha leadership within their canine order. If one does not wish to give way, trouble is inevitable.

Two German Shepherds of the same sex but of widely differing ages are less likely to cause problems. Most of my life with the breed has been with two or three sharing our home. We have tried to keep a four- to five-year age difference and, when acquiring a new dog, have alternated between dog and bitch. Taking on Kerry, as mentioned earlier, was an exception, and regretted for other reasons. A young puppy coming into our home would normally be matched with a middle-aged dog of the opposite sex and an oldie of the same sex. By the time the puppy had graduated through adolescence the oldie would be

Callum: Shadowsquad Callum of Ardfern C.D.Ex. U.D.Ex. W.D.Ex. P.D.Ex.

beyond the stage of trying to maintain Alpha status, or would have died. This policy has, I believe, ensured loyalty within the family circle

When losing a devoted canine companion, most German Shepherds have their human family to fall back on. They can overcome their loss quite quickly. Some even relish their new-found status, enjoying a higher place in the pecking order. However, we did experience one tragic situation with Callum and Jeza as our canine companions. Callum was in his tenth year when we lost him. Although inevitable, it was a tragic blow to both Irene and myself to lose such a faithful friend. Jeza had lived her life with Callum around. She was six years old at the time. She relied on Callum. He was her anchor.

About a week after Callum had gone, Jeza became seriously ill with haemorrhagic enteritis. For two days her life was in the balance. The vet considered the illness to be stress-related. Was it the loss of Callum? I do not know, but I think the vet was correct. A subordinate losing an Alpha mate may have been too much for Jeza. When she did pull through, she became a much more assertive animal. She let Callum's replacement some months later know she was now Alpha leader of the pack.

Loyalty between German Shepherds and Other Species

It is obvious that the most important and demanding relationship in this area was and is between German Shepherds and

*Puppies exploring
the concepts of
dominance and
submission.*

sheep in their home country. The development of the German Shepherd was through the various shepherding types of dog which protected the flocks of sheep from predators. The strength of loyalty and commitment, evident then, is still well ingrained within the breed. There are many instances in family life of a German Shepherd's loyalty to and protection of the family animals, particularly the dog's own cat. Gamekeepers who have German Shepherds to help deter poachers find that their dogs can even protect young chicks.

Dirk was one such Shepherd. He was a big strong dog and he had already been introduced to manwork. He was a very hard dog, yet when introduced to a gamekeeper's life at about five years of age, he could be let loose among the pheasant chicks without a thought of trouble. Young chicks often die off for no apparent reason. Peter, the gamekeeper, would take the dead chicks out of the pen and throw them to the side. Dirk would immediately pick up the dead chick and gently bring it back to Peter. These chicks became part of Dirk's flock. He would also allow the gamekeeper's cockerel to feed out of his dish, but woe betide any of the other dogs who tried to do the same.

One young German Shepherd bitch went to a farm at the age of eight weeks and was brought up with the usual array of animals as her friends. She grew up with two geese, a male and a female. The geese were devoted to each other but one day the female disappeared. Nobody knew what had happened to her; she was probably shot. The gander attached himself to the Shepherd bitch – he had found a new mate. He protected her, although she did not need it. The gander had fallen for this dog. She was quite happy to accept the relationship, and they became inseparable.

As the tracking dog, Caro takes a leading role in the partnership.

The Constituents of Loyalty

This subject takes us back to the heart of the wolf pack system. Loyalty to the pack and its leader was the foundation of their group system of existence. This is also the outlook of the German Shepherd in the environment of his human family.

The four principal constituents are:

• Dominance.
• Submission.
• Affection.
• Fear.

There are other ingredients, but they are included in the principal four.

Again we can use the commitments and feelings between human beings to illustrate the functions of these constituents. If we can understand our own emotions, we can start to understand those of our dogs – especially if we 'think German Shepherd' when looking at the interaction between people.

Various human relationships demonstrate a number of combinations of the four principal constituents of loyalty. For exam-

ple, marriage shows varying degrees and fluctuations of dominance and submission. Sometimes it is right for one partner in a relationship to take the dominant position to defend or guide the other through something he or she finds difficult. But dominance should not become a domineering attitude, and in the same way an owner with a permanently domineering attitude towards his dog does not put pleasure into a dog's life. Similarly, a reversal of roles, with the dog being the dominant and domineering partner, will certainly lead to a disastrous relationship with consequences going well beyond acceptable coexistence.

Affectionate devotion should be a very important ingredient in any marriage. It may be considered that fear should not play any part in the relationship of married couples. This is true if we consider fear of each other, but fear of offending a partner should always be a consideration.

Loyalty in other fields also shows the four principal constituents in varying degrees. The loyalty between employer and employee shows a different set of values, just as that between members of a social club brings out yet another set. In these instances loyalty is considered appropriate not for life, but for the duration of the mutual agreement. The value placed on it may well be tempered by stature or ambitions: for example, someone may have ambitions to progress up the ladder of promotion at work, or in the hierarchy in the social club. A dog may have an equally strong ambition to become the indisputable leader of his human pack. When these ambitions (human or canine) get out of hand, the importance placed on loyalty becomes less. In such cases, uncompromising dominance can result in total submission of others. Affection can then become non-existent, and fear will play a much more prominent role.

Be it human versus human or human versus dog, the regime of dominance and submission must be flexible, and properly balanced to suit the situation. Without accepting this philosophy, one cannot understand human or canine needs.

It may well be thought that man should always be the dominant partner in a relationship with his dog. It is certainly true that a dog should always respect the wishes of his master. Many dogs, including German Shepherds, will try at some time in their lives to become the dominant companion. The story of Strachan was an extreme but certainly not an isolated example. I have known many cases of a German Shepherd becoming the dominant partner. The owners, through lack of knowledge, or misplaced affection, have caused themselves a problem. In Strachan's case the problem was recognized very early and overcome. In many cases it is weakness on the part of the owner – the belief that the dog will grow out of it. This generally allows canine dominance to flourish.

Both gentle Quest and tougher Callum objected once to something that I did, and growled at me. It was the only time in their lives that they acted in this manner towards myself or a member of the family. They were both about ten months old and ready to assert their authority. A sharp – very sharp – word from myself stopped both of them in their tracks. They never did it again. They were permitted (not encouraged) to take a very dominant role in training for and qualifying in manwork. To train a dog in tracking is to train him to be the leader of the pack. This leadership by the dog is gladly taken, but he returns to a more submissive role when the job is completed.

Associated with the four principal constituents of loyalty are other ingredients. For example, we often speak of an honest dog. This is a dog you can trust. Honesty is a by-product of the 'big four' and it comes down to the dog's respect for his owner. That is surely the result of the respect the owner has for his dog. A German Shepherd with a well-balanced outlook with regard to dominance and submission, who shows devoted affection to his owner without the fear of being mistreated, will repay his companion by his completely open and honest approach to life.

Controlled canine aggression is another sign of dominance from a German Shepherd, and is appropriate when his partner requires his dog's support in a situation demanding such a response. However, there is always a fine line between controlled and uncontrolled aggression, and the German Shepherd owner must always ensure that his dog is responsible to him, rather than for him.

CHAPTER 4

Intelligence

Before discussing the intelligence of the German Shepherd we need a reasonable understanding of how our interpretation of the subject relates to the breed.

A dictionary definition of intelligence is 'the quickness of understanding with the ability to reason or deliberate'. The Breed Standard for the German Shepherd includes terms such as adaptable, tractable, trainable, essentially linked with intelligence.

Adaptability is the ability to adjust to, or harmonize with, new or changing situations; to have a degree of flexibility.

Tractability is present in dogs that are easily handled and are amenable to the leadership of their human companions.

Trainability indicates a dog's responsiveness to a standard of control; it equates to effective working ability with an eager mind.

Although ability to memorize is not mentioned either in the Standard or in the dictionary definition of intelligence, it must be a major factor in the ability to understand and therefore to reason or deliberate. The ability to retain knowledge is thus a fundamental constituent of intelligence. The ability to understand and make practical use of that knowledge is another factor. How much that affects German Shepherds is open to interpretation. It is much easier to define in human beings.

These are considered to be the elements of intelligence but that is only part of the story. The ability to understand and retain knowledge with the power to reason or deliberate has its own genetic base. Inheritance of the various senses and fields of working ability will be evident from the strengths and weaknesses in the different areas of knowledge.

It may be appropriate to look at ourselves before concentrating on the dog. Although the reasoning power of man differs greatly from that of the German Shepherd, the strengths and weaknesses can be more clearly visualized if we consider the differing kinds of intelligence shown by people. For example, a person may appear to have an extraordinary gift in one subject, but to be devoid of any real understanding in other areas of knowledge or ability. There are gifted scholars who have no idea how to change an electric plug. They would not know where to start or what tools to use. There are language experts who cannot boil an egg. It is not uncommon to be able to grasp a complex situation within one's own field of expertise, but to find it difficult to understand the rudiments of a much simpler situation in some other field.

Adaptable: from a state of aggression ...

I recall a situation at one of my domestic dog training classes where two particular clients were members of the medical profession. One, who attended with his Springer Spaniel, was a treat to instruct. He could be shown a handling technique once and he did it. He could immediately handle the situation in the manner prescribed, and his dog would always respond.

The other was an orthopaedic surgeon. Clearly, he had the intelligence to become an expert in his highly specialized field and the manual dexterity to carry out intricate operations on the human body. But when it came to handling and training his Labrador he was quite incapable of following simple instructions. I could take his dog to demonstrate the various tech-

niques, and he was at a loss to follow my example. Others could, but he could not. He would tell me that I had a hypnotic effect on his dog. I still do not know if he was serious or joking, but after a few weeks he decided to let his fourteen-year-old daughter bring the dog for instruction. The dog's response changed completely. The daughter, like me, was able to get the best out of the dog. Her father understood the theory of dog-training, but could not put it into practice.

In the days when I played golf, I had a bad slice, particularly when I used a wood off the tee. My problem was analysed and explained to me. The cure was fully explained and I understood, but putting theory into practice was a different matter. As that slice did not improve, I gave

... to that of the unconcerned bystander.

up golf for an activity that gave me much more pleasure, where I could put theory into practice – dog training.

We all have our inherited strong and weak points; with dogs it is the same. In training a German Shepherd for competition or police work there are four principal fields of ability:

- Control (Obedience).
- Agility.
- Nosework.
- Protection work.

It is commonly recognized that a Shepherd with a strong talent for protection work is unlikely to have the same quickness of understanding in nosework. Such a dog will have the intelligence to be easily trained for the various func-

tions that make a good protection dog, but may never become a top-class tracker without taxing all the skills of a good trainer to bring his nosework to a high level of competence. Each German Shepherd has his own natural levels of intelligence in various areas, but his expertise may lie dormant unless his trainer has the knowledge and ability to activate his talents.

The ability to use his inherited senses and the working characteristics of the breed is an indication of the German Shepherd's intelligence. The knowledge and ability of the trainer is also an important ingredient. I have often heard someone say that his dog is 'stupid', that he cannot do this or understand that, or that he obeys only when he feels like it. These people honestly believe that the dog is 'stupid'. In fact, the dog is far too intelligent for them to handle. The dog knows precisely what he can get away with, and can manipulate situations to his own ends.

The intelligence of German Shepherds covers many factors and this affects our assessment of individual dogs, so determining intelligence does become a matter of opinion. However, I shall try to take a balanced view to illustrate the various features that make up 'intelligence'. It would be easy to misrepresent situations by concentrating on particular lines of breeding, so the dogs used in my anecdotes will normally be from different lines of breeding. Upbringing can also affect a dog's apparent intelligence so, again, all the dogs I have chosen for my anecdotes in this chapter were brought up in my own household.

External Influences

Training for professional police work, Working Trials or Obedience changes the character of a dog and can make him seem more intelligent than he is. The ability of the trainer and the methods applied will have a direct influence on the ease of achieving a satisfactory end result. A poor trainer can ruin a dog that has a high degree of natural ability and intelligence, while a good trainer can turn a difficult and uninspiring German Shepherd into a performer to be admired.

The same situation arises in the home. Considerate ownership, with the ability to achieve disciplined behaviour, gives the dog the opportunity for a creative outlook. Inconsiderate or undisciplined ownership can either smother the dog's creativity or induce an artful or cunning response which can channel creativity and intelli-

gence into unwanted territory. Domestic upbringing and training can sometimes give a false impression of a German Shepherd's outlook on life and therefore of his inherited intelligence. There are many external factors that have an effect on dogs, as we shall see.

Reasoning Ability

Living with certain dogs and training them affords the opportunity to assess their intelligence and natural working ability. No doubt the presence of other dogs in the home also has an effect. Quest came into our home without other dogs for company, but our two daughters, aged five and ten, created a real family atmosphere, and he liked the company of the girls and their friends. I was a beginner at dog training and gave Quest a lot of attention. Although he started off as a very shy puppy, the fact that he enjoyed life made him want to do things and he showed a working ability along with intelligence which may otherwise have remained dormant. Not all German Shepherds have the same opportunities.

Two other dogs feature in these anecdotes. Tanya, our first bitch, came as a puppy when Quest was nearly three, and Callum joined us when the old boy was about ten. Dogs do learn from each other, but there are many instances when one dog does not seem to have the intelligence of others. Callum was a case in point. To generalize, I would say that Quest was reasonably intelligent, Tanya brilliant and Callum just dumb. As to working ability, or trainability, Quest was easy, Tanya was very difficult and Callum was easy to difficult depending on the field of work.

The tractable animal – one that is amenable to the attentions that make up the daily routines of health management.

Callum was a 'macho' dog. He was built like an Aberdeen Angus bull. His puppyhood has already been discussed in Chapter 2; his working attributes will be examined later. Some aspects of his day-to-day intelligence left much to be desired. For example, we could give Quest a raw egg; he would take it outside, drop it and eat it. Give Tanya an egg and she would do the same. Give Callum an egg at the same time as the others and he would take it outside, place it gently on the ground and look at it. Tanya had watched and learnt from Quest, but Callum just looked. Eventually we would break it for him. Now was that unintelligent, or did he learn to appear unintelligent so that we would break the egg for him?

At this time, before the days of BSE, I would sometimes buy an ox head to feed the dogs good red meat. I would bone the head and get some ten to twelve pounds of cheek and trimmings. By sawing the back off the head I could also get about a pound of nourishing brain, while the cut-off snout was a juicy morsel for a dog to chew away at. The three sections of head would be thrown on to the back yard for the three dogs. Quest knew what he was doing and would go for the snout. Callum, being the 'macho' dog, went for the large middle section, leaving Tanya with the small back piece of the head. Tanya also loved to have the eyes in the middle section and evolved her own crafty approach to getting it. She would walk away, go round the side of the house to the back gate and bark. Callum would rush round to see what she was barking at and pass Tanya, by now on her way back to secure

A potential escape artist?

the centre part of the head. This happened time and time again: Callum never twigged. He was caught every time by an artful and cunning female. He would never try to take the head from Tanya, and had to settle for the small back piece.

I do not think it took much intelligence on Callum's part to outwit Jeza. She replaced Tanya after she had died. Callum was four years old and Jeza six months when she joined our family. She was a quiet, inoffensive pup. Having had a rather unhappy beginning to her life (this was her fourth home already), she was stressed and very uncertain of her surroundings. Her first day and her first meal of ox-cheek and biscuit were an eye-opener. Jeza picked out the pieces of meat one at a time and buried them in various parts of the garden. She did not realize

that Callum was following her, digging up each piece she had buried. Callum was not so dumb after all. His quickness of understanding came to the surface during his training sessions. He may not have shown the initiative to work out the solution to a problem like some of our other dogs, but he could learn and understand what was wanted when he was taken through a particular situation.

One example was when we took Callum with us for a walk over the new River Tay road bridge. About a mile out from the Dundee side was an observation platform with an open metal spiral staircase leading to the viewing station. Callum at first refused to go up these stairs, but with gentle coaxing and encouragement he took it step by step right to the top. There was a beautiful view both up and down the river, although it could be unnerving to look down at the swirling currents of water below. Finally we descended and, while still on the lead, I asked Callum to go up again. He responded without a second thought.

The sequel to this story came some two weeks later, when we were competing at a rally organized by the Scottish Working Trials Society. It was held in the main arena at the Royal Highland Show Ground on the outskirts of Edinburgh. The judges were practical dog-handlers from Edinburgh City Police and the 'Send away' test was up the open spiral staircase to the commentary box. Callum was the only dog to do the test to the judge's full satisfaction. Some would not even attempt the first step and others would go to the first bend, look down and, as if to say 'This is not for me', would come down again. Callum would have been no better than the rest without his earlier experience; but he had remembered.

Memory and Delayed Response

Delayed response is the ability to memorize an event and make use of it later. Memory and delayed response thus go together, and are very important functions of intelligence. In this respect dogs are no different from human beings. If an event is important enough to us, we remember it, even if it happens only once. For example, one dishonest action on the part of a trusted friend or partner may be forgiven but not forgotten. The date of one's own birthday, learned as a child, is always remembered. I visit a nursery from time to time and on one occasion I offered the owner's old black Labrador a liver treat from a box I keep in my pocket. Being a typical Lab, he enjoyed his tit-bit and never forgot. Every subsequent visit brought the old boy to his feet and over with a friendly paw looking for his treat.

A dog learns just as effectively from an unpleasant act, connecting it with the cause of the unpleasantness. He is unlikely to blame himself. He will blame the car tailgate if his tail or ear has been caught in it at some time in the past, and will make sure it never happens again. If he has been slapped for failing to return when called, he will remember that slap 'for coming back' and will be reluctant to return the next time. Loyalty will be mixed with apprehension, until apprehension takes full control.

Intelligence through memory has many other aspects. A repeated sequence of activities preceding a particular event will eventually lead the dog to anticipate what is going to follow. Training is based on repeating an activity until the dog has connected it in his mind with the need to respond in the required manner. The number of times the action has to be repeated for the dog to fully memorize the situation will vary.

This is not only one of the principles of training, but also a general principle of canine learning. For example, the dog's master picks up his shoes to put on, and his dog is there waiting to go out for a walk. The master picks up the dog's dish, and the dog is there waiting for his meal. The master picks up the grooming equipment and the dog is nowhere to be found because he knows and does not like it. There are many such everyday situations where the dog's intelligence tells him what is going to happen next.

The ability to read a situation and work out a solution to the problem it has creat-

Digger will not forget the little boy who teased him ...

ed is where real intelligence comes in. In the case of Tanya and the ox-head, the thinking behind her deliberate actions to draw Callum away from the part of the head she wanted showed intelligence with a cunning streak. Could that have been inherited from her ancestors the wolves, where the females would do anything to get food for their young? It is possible.

Territorial knowledge is an important area of memory which could be a relic from the past. Wolves seem to carry a ground plan of their territory in their heads. When taken out of their territory on a chase or a hunt for food, they have no difficulty in finding their way back. Females with pups, in particular, would have an added incentive to find their way back to the den. They had to ensure the survival of the next generation. I have watched my own dogs – the bitches, in particular – when we are on holiday. Taken once for a walk, from the caravan or car, they instinctively know the exact route they took on the outward journey and follow it back home. Once, on a visit into town on a busy Saturday afternoon when we took Tanya with us, she led the way back. She crossed roads at the same places we crossed on the outward journey. It was uncanny to watch such a precise memory guiding us back to the car. This was not done by nosework. There was no doubt that her eyes were controlling her actions.

Quest spent his first four years in Scotland before we moved to the south of England. Broughty Ferry was always home to him and during our five years in

... but he does have a gentler side.

England we returned to our roots every summer. On our journeys north, Quest would recognize 'home' territory a little further away from Broughty each time. On the last journey, when we resettled back in Broughty, Quest sat up as we were going through Glen Farg, some thirty-five (56km) miles from our destination. As he had been lying down and could not see the surroundings, I assume that he recognized the scent in the air. Whatever it was that told him, he sat and watched for the rest of the journey.

Fortunately, German Shepherds are more tied to home than many other breeds and are therefore less inclined than some to wander. However, there are many tales of dogs being lost while they are outside their normal territory, then finding their way home. Our own dogs very rarely had the opportunity to be mislaid, even for a very short period of time. I can think of only three occasions. Panic set in on each of them. They proved to be minor instances, but when our dogs are out of sight and not responding immediately, it is a worry.

When training for a specific exercise, repeated events will enable Tegan to memorize what is required of her.

One situation involved Callum. We had just moved from the south of England back to Scotland and it was our first day in our new home. We were moving in when suddenly we realized that six-month-old Callum was missing. With all the coming and going, the front gate had been left open.

There was a farmhouse with outbuildings and a small field across the road, but there was no sign of him scavenging there. Irene and I went in opposite directions along the street. He was only two houses away, standing at the back door waiting to be let in. He was close, but his senses or intelligence were not sufficiently developed to enable him to find his way back to his new home. I would like to think it was just a sign of his lack of maturity at the time.

Success and Failure

Dogs will learn through activities that, in their minds, result in success or failure. German Shepherds, in particular, will learn very quickly. Success is pleasant and failure is unpleasant. It depends on the degree whether it is really meaningful to the dog or not.

Let us go back to nature and the wolf. Suppose that, while in search of food, a wolf tackles a large, fit and healthy animal and gets badly injured. He will remember, then think seriously before tackling such a beast in the future. Failure will stick firmly in his mind; it was a very unpleasant experience. To have challenged a similar animal that was obviously old and infirm, where success had resulted in a full stomach, would have been a very pleasant experience, especially if he had been very hungry. It could even have been life-saving. Success and failure result in satisfaction or disappointment. How quickly a dog learns depends on his intelligence and the effect of the experience.

Dogs will always learn faster and more easily if they think they have caused their own experiences. The result is immediate. The case of the wolf is obvious, but if a dog's ear or tail gets accidentally caught in the tailgate of the car, it hurts, it is instantaneous, and a sensible dog will never let it happen again. So long as he does not connect it with human interference, unpleasant situations will not be blamed on us. Pleasant canine experiences are another matter. As far as possible, we should want such experiences to be credited to ourselves. That is one reason why dogs stay with us: we give them security and they feel dependent on us.

There are, of course, many occasions when we have no alternative but to create an unpleasant situation to counter an undesirable act. Once, with Callum, I felt it necessary to take drastic action. I had unintentionally helped to create the conditions that caused the problem. We had moved to our new home in Broughty and I had taken the gate from the end of the drive and brought it back in line with the front of the house, to keep the dogs out of the front garden and away from the road. The front wall was only about two feet

(60cm) high. Unfortunately this allowed the occasional stray dog to enter the front driveway and garden. As the gate was only three feet (90cm) in height, Callum found no difficulty in clearing it to chase a stray out of 'his' garden. He did this, crossed the road and chased the dog quite a distance. Although the road was quiet at that time it was sometimes busy with people going to and from work. This was an accident waiting to happen if something was not done.

I had compounded the problem by allowing Callum to welcome me home from work each day by putting his feet on top of the gate. This was obviously the first stage towards jumping over. The day after he chased the dog out of our garden, I put a plan into action. I came home from work and got out of the car. Callum came to the gate and jumped up as usual to put his feet on top. I thumped his feet very hard with both fists clenched. He withdrew and put his forefeet back on the ground. I then praised him. He thought about jumping up again; I used a very strong 'No', and he responded. I never had to take such strong physical action again. A word or a look was sufficient to keep him from jumping on the gate again, and he never attempted to jump over it after that. It was a hard lesson, and it was not his fault, but it was a life-saver. He could have been killed on the road, or could have caused injury or death to an innocent motorist.

Pleasantness and unpleasantness are the key instruments in the process of learning. In the case just described, Callum experienced extreme unpleasantness on that one occasion. A slower and less unpleasant route could have been taken with the same end result – but we could not afford to wait. When life and limb are at stake, the shortest possible route becomes essential, so long as it is followed up by a period of consolidation and reinforcing the new rule.

This is where pleasantness and consolidation come in. Each evening on my return from work Callum was allowed to come to the gate to welcome me (to have kept him in the house at that time would deprive me of the opportunity to consolidate the harder lesson with a more kindly approach). He would welcome me home and I would respond with equal enthusiasm. A positive 'No', delivered at the correct time, prevented him from getting beyond the thinking stage of putting his paws on the gate. An immediate and lengthy follow-up of praise and fondling, with the gate between us, created the reward through pleasantness. My delight, shown to the extreme, gave Callum the fullest satisfaction under controlled conditions.

Another aspect of intelligence counters the view, held by many dog trainers and behaviourists, that dogs must learn from single-word commands. Admittedly such an approach while competing in Obedience competitions is a necessity; but for day-to-day living and most aspects of work the dog will enjoy being asked in a less formal manner.

As all my dogs have competed in Obedience and Working Trials, my approach to 'educating' them has been mixed. On occasions a single word instruction would be the end result of a training procedure, on others, a sentence or a phrase would be used to achieve the desired response. For a recall the single word 'Come', along with his name, would be applied. Sending him in to the search square, I would say, 'You go and find it son'. (For a bitch I would use 'lass'.) This approach is based on the belief that dogs

learn from actions not words. They then connect these actions with specific noises and consequently can respond to a variety of messages for a single activity.

An example is the alternative approaches I can use to have Ceilidh sit. She was initially induced to sit in front of me by drawing her head up to receive a tit-bit. As her head came up she automatically sat and received her reward. During the same period she was taught to sit at my left side by physical pressure. She was then induced to accept the meaning of the word 'Sit' after she had learned to anticipate my actions and sit before I had the opportunity to complete the process. The development continued from working close-up to sitting at a distance from me, with instructions being varied from time to time. She now sits to the following commands or gestures:

1. I say 'Sit' at any time.
2. I use the whistle (usually at a distance).
3. I give a hand signal, sometimes at a distance.
4. I draw myself up to my full height, normally when she is close to me.
5. I use the phrase 'What's your bottom for?' (This was initially used to have her sit at the edge of the pavement before we crossed a road. It is now used to amuse the children who think it is funny. She will sit for them when they say it.)
6. On occasions a combination of the above are used as I see fit.

Each variation has just developed through time and shows the intelligence of our breed in their ability to cope with many different instructions for the same activity. I do not believe Ceilidh is so special and I am sure many pet German Shepherds would do as well if given the opportunity. The dog's limitations are in the hands of the owners. Kennel dogs do not have the same opportunity to gain the variety of experiences and consequently cannot show the full potential of their inheritance. However, I doubt if any of us have the ability to maximize a dog's mental capabilities to their full potential.

Intelligence – the influential factors

A number of factors will determine the intelligence of your dog. Some of these are beyond anyone's control – genetic inheritance being the most obvious. However, the way in which a dog will use his intelligence can be influenced by us; and, with the German Shepherd (as with human beings), exercise for his brain is essential if he is not to become bored and, ultimately, less apparently intelligent. Some tips on keeping your dog interested and challenged, outside of the formal training session, might be:

Activity Toys
There are various activity toys that can be used to test a dog's intelligence and to amuse him for a period. My own preference is for the acitivity ball: your dog may even learn to pick it up.

Fun Retrieve
Retrieving can lead to so many different functions that give great pleasure to German Shepherds and can be very useful in everyday life.

- Fun retrieving is easily turned into fun searching for articles that you have thrown or put into the undergrowth.

- It is also the basis for 'seek-backs' for an articles – a bunch of keys or a glove – which has been 'accidentally dropped. While out for a walk, see how far your dog will track the way you have come to find your dropped article.

- Hide and seek: you do the hiding, and your Shepherd tries to find you. While out for a walk, hide behind a tree, bush, or other suitably positioned obstacle, when your dog is not looking. Then wait until he finds you. This is a great way of teaching your Shepherd to keep an eye on you.

None of these activities and games need to be done to competition standard. They are merely a means of using your Shepherd's inheritance for his enjoyment and yours. Having said that, you never know when they may have a practical use. Training details can be found in my books, *Training the German Shepherd Dog* and *Your Dog* (*see* Further Reading).

CHAPTER 5

Steadiness of Nerves

The term 'steadiness of nerves' is often used to mean the same as temperament. It is certainly one of many factors that play a major role in the temperament of a German Shepherd. However, steadiness of nerves is more accurately described in terms of courage or self-confidence. Determination and leadership qualities are other closely related factors. Self-control is another important factor in the genetic make-up of any member of a breed so renowned for its guarding and protection capabilities.

Genetic Factors and Upbringing

No dog or breeding line is perfect. In breeding, any lines with known strengths or weaknesses should be fully understood and accepted for what they are. This will help to produce the most suitable dog for a particular purpose and environment.

Although German Shepherds are renowned for their all-round capabilities, there are lines of breeding that lend themselves to particular functions. There are, of course, individual dogs that have exceptional ability in some particular field of work, yet whose breeding gives no indication of these abilities. Many dormant talents remain undiscovered because the owners do not have the knowledge or ability to awaken these qualities.

Environmental background can upset the assessment of any dog's genetic contribution to the breed's future. Without knowledge of a dog's parentage and the behaviour of his siblings, it can be difficult to tell what influence breeding has had. Genetic inheritance can be the making of a dog, but inappropriate upbringing can be his ruin.

I recall visiting a breeder to view a German import with the thought of having a puppy from him at some time in the future. I will call him Arno. We viewed him from outside the kennel run. There were four of us and the breeder watching him and he looked quite relaxed and natural. As a test, I started to move quite furtively, crouching and darting behind my companions. Arno began to look very uncertain. He retreated towards his kennel. His body movements and the look of distrust in his eyes showed that he was decidedly uneasy about my actions.

Arno was still a youngster and had gained his Schutzhund I before leaving Germany. Recognizing that he had the freshness of youth, I asked the breeder whether he had been pushed through his Schutzhund. He replied that he was surprised at Arno's attitude and that he had never reacted like that before. I asked whether the dog had ever been tested

These four puppies in the same litter will all have variations in genetic abilities which ensures that they are all different – four individuals.

before. He had not, and it appeared that he had been pushed through his Schutzhund qualification before he was sold.

We then took Arno out of his run, to find that he was at ease again. He had regained his self-assurance and was a real pleasure to be with. That little quirk in his nature, that momentary lack of confidence, was not inherited. It was caused by inappropriate training in his home country to achieve a higher export price at an early age. Otherwise this youngster proved to have a well-balanced character. His steadiness of nerves had been made suspect by environmental conditioning. Another youngster with a stronger inherited character may well have gone through such training without any adverse effect.

Confidence

Many dogs must be cultivated, encouraged and developed to give them confidence, especially if protection work is to be part of their training. Dogs of a softer nature have to be nurtured.

Quest was an example of this. (I have already given some background about his introduction to our family in Chapter 2.) Genetically, he had a very quiet and retiring nature, and the low-key, secluded atmosphere in which he'd spent his first eight weeks of life did him no favours. An early assessment of him could have been 'shy'. With my present knowledge and experience, I would probably ignore such a puppy in favour of a more outgoing specimen – but then I

Quest – the canine gentleman who became a W.T. Champion.

would have missed out on a great friend and partner who started me on a career that took over my life.

When Quest did come out of his shell he led a life of confidence, and had the courage to make his name in police work in Kennel Club Working Trials. However, he was always the 'gentleman', even when he gained the status of W.T. Champion.

This highlights the important point

that German Shepherds are trained to protect. Although Quest was a fairly soft dog, he was not nervous, and he was a well-adjusted adult of some three years old when we started in this field of training. Encouraging a nervous dog to protect or defend can be a very dangerous approach. It can bring so many uncertainties and doubts into a dog's mind. His lack of confidence can create a lack of judgement on his part, and he may attack at the most inopportune moment and for the wrong reasons.

Quest's early Working Trials career had been very successful, but it was very difficult to move on into the next stage of competition unless we were prepared to consider Police Dog (P.D.) Open Stakes. The only alternative was Tracker Dog (T.D.) Open Stakes, but they were not run in Scotland during those early years. As it was a 1,000-mile (1,600km) round trip to compete in the nearest T.D. Stake, it was P.D. or nothing.

It was suggested that we train for P.D. There was only one Trials event a year in Scotland and we would miss out completely if we did not train for it. However, with two young daughters and their friends about the house, I was reluctant. To move into the side of work that encouraged aggressiveness in a dog was a big decision. Jim Whytock, my mentor, persuaded me to watch the training and give it a try. 'If you don't like it, we won't go any further,' he said. 'You have seen my dog at work and play, also Jack Grant's – they are both perfectly safe.'

Their approach was more of a game, a confidence-building exercise with strict control over the dog's reactions. Quest was a 'gentleman'; he enjoyed the rough and tumble, but it took some time to get a good solid bite. He was never a hard biter,

and always seemed to be apologizing for taking a bite. Eventually Quest did many demonstrations in front of the public. As 'criminals' worked to toughen him up during training, he gained more confidence and became more effective. However, he could be taken off the field immediately after doing his 'protection' work and go into a crowd of children to be patted and cuddled by all.

Callum was different. This puppy was born with more confidence than he knew what to do with. The breeder warned me that he would have a 'gay' tail. This could affect his movement and consequently his show career. It was really a sign of his cockiness. As described in Chapter 2, when he got over his short spell of uncertainty as a juvenile, he returned to his full arrogance. Fortunately he did understand his place within the family, and he did give some respect to Quest, but the old boy was no real challenge. Tanya was different, a dominant bitch, and Callum knew where to draw the line.

A handler can give a dog tremendous confidence in tracking by backing him all the way. However, confidence is easily destroyed and if the handler nags or is inconsistent in approach, he can create much uncertainty in the dog's mind. A handler or owner's lack of confidence will certainly rub off on his dog.

There was one competitor who was highly successful in Working Trials, but at one very important event his German Shepherd failed in one particular exercise. His wife's comment was that he had 'sorted the dog out'. It was obvious that the 'sorting out' had put the dog into a highly stressed state of mind and the dog, who was normally self-assured, with plenty of confidence, lost all his composure that day. The handler's attitude was

Quest giving a demonstration of protection work with our mentor acting as criminal.

not the least bit forgiving. His body language and facial expression told the dog he was not man's best friend at that moment. The dog was looking for some sort of recognition. He wanted to please, but his confidence had been stripped away. He was too busy worrying about his master's next unpredictable move to concentrate on the work that was to follow. His confusion led to further mistakes.

Unfortunately handlers in this state of mind do not, at the time, see the damage they are doing. These situations generally have a long-term effect on the confidence the dog has in himself and in the future relationship of the working partnership.

Courage

Courage in the life of a German Shepherd is more about defence than attack. Does he have the spirit or resolution to stand by his owner in times of need? Does he have the courage to cope with the rigours of police or security work?

When chasing a criminal, the dog's real purpose is to apprehend rather than to aggressively attack with the conscious intention of causing bodily harm. The objective in apprehending is to catch, hold and keep on holding the suspect under all circumstances until the dog's handler is in a position to take charge of the situation.

Tara shows courage in defence of her owner.

Any dog with true courage will have a fair degree of natural confidence, but many dogs show false courage. Any dog (or person, for that matter) can seem to be courageous when he is really just a big bully. So-called courage can be a cover for fear; a show of aggression can easily be misinterpreted by an owner as a sign of courage. We have even seen a working police dog being chased off the field by a 'criminal' during the test of courage at a Working Trials.

Callum was one dog who showed great courage. At two-and-a-half years of age he had qualified through the grades of competition within Working Trials in preparation for the Police Dog (P.D.) Stake. During training for this very demanding stake we discovered that he had one extremely bad hip. I was going to retire him there and then, but eventually I accepted the vet's suggestion that he be given cortisone treatment for the short period of the trials. Callum gave a number of indications of his courage at that

event, but one situation in particular is worthy of mention here.

Experience and a gradual build-up of training would give the best chance of qualifying in this work, but because of his age, experience was not on Callum's side. The test of courage that Callum undertook that day was carried out by leaving him in the 'Down' position while the handler went of sight. The 'criminal' then appeared with a stick and walk over to the dog in a furtive, then threatening, manner. He stood in front of the dog waving the stick and threatening him. At this provocation the dog should get up, and then either attack or take evasive action (possibly by circling the 'criminal'). Whatever his reaction, the dog should maintain contact with the 'criminal'. If possible, the 'criminal' would hit the dog as often as necessary on the shoulder with the (very flexible) stick to test his reactions. This allows the judge to assess the dog's courage while under attack.

Callum's inexperience was evident during this test. He did not know what to do;

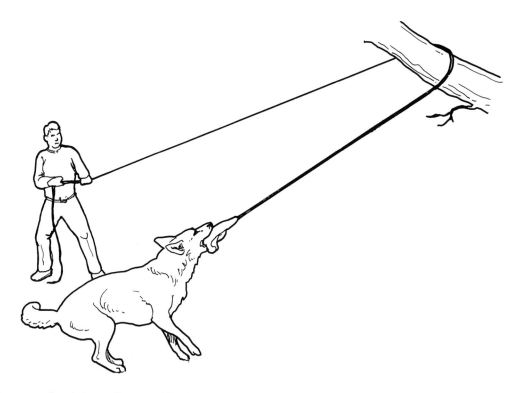

A means of training a German Shepherd to develop a good solid bite without using a 'criminal'.

his master had left him in the 'Down' position, and from his previous training he felt that he was under instruction to stay in that position. The 'criminal's' frenzied attack confused him. He was uncertain; he had always trusted his master that no harm would come to him when left at the 'Down'.

Eventually he stood up but did not move away. Then came the beating, on both right and left shoulders. It stung, but that was all. It was a light flexible stick, which then broke. At that point, Callum decided it was his turn. Without any hesitation, he went straight in for the right arm, held on and completely immobilized the 'criminal'. I was then called back to end the exercise. Although he wore a protective sleeve, the 'criminal's' arm bore the evidence of Callum's retaliation. He was awarded full marks for the test of courage. Under unusual and difficult circumstances for him, Callum's inherited attributes took over and won the day. He was a very hard dog, but honest and well balanced in the characteristics that make up the requirements for steadiness of nerves.

Leadership

Genetically speaking, courage, confidence and determination go hand in hand. Leadership is a more complicated factor.

The strength of the bite required to hold a 'criminal'.

Although great strength in one of the first three qualities normally ensures that the other two are at a high level, sometimes ownership and handling distort the balance. Good and considerate handling will, in itself, control or manipulate a dog's outlook on leadership.

During normal domestic situations leadership must be taken over by the owner, with the dog being prepared to play second fiddle. However, when he is looking after the house, while alone, or when his owner is in bed for the night, he is expected to take the lead in warning of intruders. Although there are some situations in a domestic environment when dogs should be allowed to take over, there are many others where this will introduce serious problems.

Working German Shepherds come into a different category. There are occasions when the dogs are conditioned to take the lead and to make their own decisions. Protection work, searching and tracking are examples. The dogs are trained to carry out such functions without unwarranted interference from their handlers. In those situations the handlers are there to initiate and terminate the procedures, also to give the dog moral support if and when necessary.

Apart from Quest, Callum was the only dog I took into the P.D. Stake in Working Trials. I was fortunate to have worked Quest in this field and had a fair amount of experience. Callum, one of the hardest dogs I had ever seen, had a grip like a vice. The longer he held, the stronger it became. There was no doubting his determination or his leadership when he was allowed to be boss. However, he did understand commands and the need to obey. Callum had no difficulty in applying self-control and would never go 'over the top'.

Although Callum was hard he was honest and responsive except during one exercise. This was the running recall, where the dog chased the 'criminal' only to be recalled just before he finalized his attack. During training Callum always ignored the recall on the first run of the day. He had to take his man. He would always respond for the rest of the session, but the first run of every training session was the same. No matter how we handled it, he would go straight for the right arm and crunch. He was always so pleased with himself. He would look at me as if to say, 'O.K., I've had my fun, now we'll do it your way.' I could not get through to him that in competition there is only one run at the exercise.

Callum only competed once in P.D.; his bad hip finished a promising career. That day, the running recall was a long one at the end of a set of hard tests. He was over 200 yards (180m) away and going strong when I gave the call with everything I could: 'Callum, Leave!' He stopped, turned and just waited for me to call him back. It was the only time he ever responded to my call. I think his hip was bothering him and he was glad to be called off. He qualified 'Excellent' and took second place against some strong competition.

Bitches

The qualities that contribute to steadiness of nerves are just as important to bitches of the breed. However, there are two other factors that affect bitches and rather complicate matters. These are protection of the nest and hormone imbalance.

Although male dogs generally have a strong instinct for protection, the instinct of bitches is more finely tuned. Because of this, their self-control often seems to be non-existent. Although this stems from her role in guarding the nest and a litter of pups, it will also apply to her human family along with their possessions, house, car etc.

Encouragement to defend without the application of controls is likely to create a dangerous weapon with a mind of its own. With some bitches, the same situation can develop without encouragement. Fortunately most bitches in a sensible household learn, as they mature, to control their instincts and give nothing more than warnings.

Of my own bitches, Tanya caused a few problems in this respect. She was probably about five to six months old when she took our grocer in full flight at the back door while he made a delivery. We were lucky: he was a personal friend and she did no damage. On another occasion, at about the same time, our younger daughter Joyce was playing in the garden with some friends. There was the usual hilarity of eight-year-olds playing. Tanya was in the house to give the children freedom to play in peace, and must have heard the commotion outside. Somebody had left the back door open and she was out in a flash to join in the fun. She got overexcited and nipped one of the girls on the backside. She was looking after her Joyce.

In the years to follow I would take Tanya with me when I was training, competing and giving demonstrations in protection work with Quest. On one such trip, she was left in the car with a window open for air circulation and the excitement became too great for her. She got out of the window and was on the field 'helping' Quest before we realized she had escaped.

Although always sharp and ready to defend, Tanya was a lovely family dog. I don't think she ever mellowed, but she did act more responsibly with age.

Kerry, Quest's daughter, was so different. Her story is related in Chapter 2 and I think her problems were principally to do with her inherited temperament, but there may have been an element of hormone imbalance. With Quest and Tanya in the house, Kerry was at the bottom of the pecking order. Any pup would be happy to have nice, gentle Quest for a father. Tanya, being a very dominant bitch, was not going to be challenged by this quiet little thing. There was no aggravation between Tanya and the puppy; she was only too happy to adopt Tanya as her mother.

There was no doubt that both Jeza and Ceilidh had hormone problems. This is a subject I do not understand. Experience may have helped me to be able to explain and appreciate the effects, but understanding the causes, or how bitches feel, is beyond me. I don't think I am the only male in this position. I recall discussing the subject with one breeder, who scoffed at my remark on hormone problems. She said that she could have eight bitches at any one time in her kennels and had never seen any real problems. 'I've had a lot more bitches through my hands than you have,' she concluded. 'I should know what I'm talking about.'

Other breeders may say the same. They may have experience of breeding problems, with false pregnancies and the like. But training can bring to light so many other situations that do not happen to 'normal' bitches. It took time for me to realize what was wrong with Jeza. I could not understand her moods. She was about two years of age and I was building up training for trials at Grantham, some 350 miles (560km) from home. Her tracking had been slow to develop but she was now coming along nicely. However, her enthusiasm was beginning to wane and I could not understand why. I thought of calling off the Grantham trials but I had also planned to show her at Peterborough the same week, so we made the trip. She did well at the show but her tracking and searching effort at the trials was beyond belief. I apologized to the judge and asked to be excused from the remainder of the work.

I had discussed Jeza's problem with our vet and he agreed that there may be hormone problems. She had been getting gradually worse and Grantham was some five weeks after the end of her season. I had given our Scottish trials at Dundee an entry the week after Grantham, just for support. There seemed to be a change in her outlook to life, so I decided to work her. The day of tracking was nine weeks after she would have been mated. She was a completely different dog. She worked a complicated track beautifully. Her problems had gone. After each season the pattern was the same. At least I now knew how to handle it, and she took a break from training after every season. A litter of pups made no difference, and she finally lived a life of leisure. My bitches always seem to get the better of me.

Like Jeza, Ceilidh was never bothered by false pregnancies but she certainly had problems. Her first season, at exactly six months old, brought a change in character. Her puppy training had been going well, but even the early desire to retrieve was

Even with her problems Ceilidh enjoyed life.

lost in moodiness. She did not want to do anything constructive. Although she did come out of that, the moodiness always returned around season time. Even after she was spayed, at about eighteen months, it took many years for it to fade into the background. Just as with Jeza, there was one trials where she just did not want to track or search, and I was ashamed of her attitude. A few months later, however, at her next trials, she worked like a beaver: a beautiful track and a lovely round of work. We did a few Obedience shows and although she seemed to enjoy the company, she could never repeat the heel work of training sessions.

Ceilidh was retired from competition work before she was three years old, not because of her problems, but through my own health problems. Her character changed through the years, and her working ability would have overcome her earlier handicaps. Yet her feeding was a factor that always puzzled us. For quite some time she went off most foods except dog biscuits. It seemed that the lower the protein value of a particular food, the better the chance of her eating it. After about five years of her life, her eating became more normal.

Controlled and Uncontrolled Aggression

It should go without saying that, for owners or handlers to utilize their dogs' inherited protective instincts, they must fully accept their responsibility towards the community. This applies as much to the general public as it does to professional security or police authorities. There is no doubt that a well-trained police dog that can mix with the public is a credit to his breed, and there are many of them. However, dogs that are permitted, encouraged or trained to show aggression are only as safe as the situations they are put into, and as safe as the owners' ability to manage them. Sometimes dogs are put into positions where accidents will happen. One such situation was publicized a number of years ago.

A police dog and handler – I will call them Marco and Ken – were patrolling the perimeter of a football field during a well-attended senior match. The strip of grass between the by-line and the crowd being patrolled was very narrow. The sergeant in charge of the operation had complained to his superior about the dangers of patrolling such a narrow strip but was told to get on with it.

At one stage in the match, the linesman ran towards Marco and Ken. As he reached them he threw his arm up, with flag in hand, to indicate an infringement. The dog anticipated an attack and flew at the raised arm. The dog was doing what he had been trained to do – defending himself and his handler. After that day, there was no more patrolling in that confined area. The dangers had been obvious to the men who worked with dogs but not to the people who managed them from an office.

It is so easy to encourage canine aggression for defensive purposes and then fail to maintain the essential control. In such cases, leadership has been surrendered by the owner and willingly accepted by the dog. To make matters worse, the owners of some shy or nervous dogs try to mask their dog's failings. They claim that their dogs are just being naturally protective, that they have courage and self-confidence.

It is important for supporters of the breed to discuss cases of uncontrolled aggression. Acknowledging problems may not always be popular, but embarrassing situations do develop and they will not go away if we just ignore their existence.

Part of the problem comes down to breeding. However, in many cases it is the environmental factors that play the greatest part, especially the attitude or behaviour of the owner. There are three main types of owner who are likely to have problems:

1. The owner who tries, but fails, to control a determined dog that has a strong desire for leadership.
2. The owner who is willing to surrender his or her responsibilities to the dog.
3. The owner who encourages a protective attitude in the dog without the knowledge or ability to apply the control that is so essential.

The borderline between maintaining control and having a canine anarchist is very fine, even in dogs with the most stable of characters.

One such situation concerned a dog of immense character, a lovely dog who could normally be trusted. He was a large, handsome, long-coated animal by the name of Hustler. He was a police dog with a good all-round working record, and was competing in Working Trials at the same time as Quest. Both dogs had qualified very well at the same trials when competing for their U.D.Ex. Now both of them were competing together for their P.D.Ex. title.

After the control and nosework groups of exercises at this event, Kevin, Hustler's handler, came up to me and said, 'Well John, we're leading the field. You have only lost one mark and I have lost two. We're well ahead of the rest.'

I replied, 'It's between us, then, if we both qualify.'

We wished each other the best of luck. Although there was a championship ticket for the winner, there was no feeling of rivalry between us. We were both relatively new to the game, and it was the qualifying that meant so much to us. To win would be a big bonus.

For the patrol group of exercises, Quest and I were called first and did quite a competent job. Quest was not the most enterprising of workers in this section and, although we finished with a decent qualifying mark, I was sure that Hustler would do better and take first place. However, he came on to the field looking for trouble. He knew the routine and was eager to get on with it; but during the exercises where he had to go in for the bite his aggression became uncontrollable. Every time Hustler went in he would refuse to come out on command. He was really enjoying himself. Kevin had to go in and physically pull his dog off the 'criminal'. This was a failure in the patrol section, and a complete waste of all his earlier good work. He had failed to qualify.

I spoke to Kevin after the event, and he accepted full responsibility for his dog's failure. He explained that during training the previous week, he and his hard-working helpers, without realizing it, had allowed the dog to take control. They had crossed that very fine line and allowed Hustler to become an irresponsible leader. It would take time and work to regain the control that was so essential for a working police dog.

Circumstances can create their own problems. Having a house dog eager to protect requires a balanced approach – an approach that many owners and dogs can't match up to. From time to time the breeding of German Shepherds changes. If breeders are not careful, we can have too many dogs that are just 'windy' or we can have too many that are hard and uncompromising. Whatever their purposes in breeding, the majority of their stock goes into the homes of the general public. One problem dog is one too many, especially if the owners do not appreciate their responsibilities. We must also accept that there are breeders who give little thought to this problem. They have much to answer for.

In my training classes, or individual consultations over the years, there have been many instances of 'windy' or uncompromising dogs getting into trouble. One case that went to court involved a two-year-old German Shepherd, Ricky, who had been taken in by his owners straight from the nest at eight weeks. He was now accused of biting a stranger. I was asked by the defence counsel to assess the dog's character.

Very important evidence against the dog had come from the two police officers who had gone to the owner's house to deliver the charge. The senior policeman made it clear that his meeting with Ricky was a very frightening experience. The dog had kept coming at him, snarling and snapping until he asked the owner to put the dog out of the room. According to the policeman, the owner had to give quite a number of commands to gain control. The policeman said in court that Ricky was a very dangerous animal. The

Quest applying self-control when it is required.

who continued to ignore him. As a deliberate and testing ploy I stood up and nonchalantly took off my jerkin. Ricky made a frightened and noisy, but aggressive, retreat. This dog was going to attack only if he was cornered or if he was sure that his adversary appeared vulnerable.

Although we became the best of friends by the end of my visit, Ricky was probably a dog of the most dangerous kind. He was weak in character, a nervous dog that had been allowed to take control. His master could exercise authority but had allowed and, probably, encouraged the dog's protective instincts without realizing that he would have to manage the situations that were bound to develop.

Ricky had been brought up in a country atmosphere and was usually walked across the neighbouring fields. He met nobody and was therefore no trouble to anybody, but one day the owner visited a market garden next to his home. As usual, Ricky was not on the lead. When the door to the shop was opened Ricky bounded out and, without the owner's noticing, jumped on another customer who was making his way into the shop. This man and his wife, a witness, claimed that Ricky had bitten him on the back. He went to hospital, where it was verified that there were two marks on his back about three inches (7.5cm) apart. The evidence from all witnesses was condemning this dog as a biter.

The fact was that Ricky had jumped up at the man. The man had turned to avoid the dog, and as a result two of Ricky's claws had gone down his back leaving the two weals that were mistaken for tooth-marks. As no teeth in a German Shepherd's mouth could have been responsible for such weals in that area of the back, the charge was reduced

policewoman who had accompanied him had also been scared and was of the same opinion. Their evidence alone created a very damaging picture.

My own experience of the dog on visiting the house was similar. Ricky certainly objected very strongly to my visit. He barked, but kept near to his master. If I moved, he backed away and barked. It was clear to me that fear and protective instincts were driving this dog. To show any sign of fear would only encourage a dog like this. To ignore him was the answer. However, the two police officers had shown fear, and Ricky had cornered them. I had refused to look at him, and he required an anchor: his master.

When I sat down and started to discuss the problem with his owners, Ricky ventured forward to investigate this stranger to 'being out of control' and the owner found guilty. I just hope the owner had learned from his mistakes.

Another situation involved a Shepherd that was hard by nature. Spike had courage, confidence in himself, determination, and the composure of a leader. His one failing was lack of self-control.

I met Spike when I was judging in Zimbabwe. We had arrived at our host's the previous evening, and were in the garden when Spike, the male German Shepherd in the household, brushed past me. I had not seen him before, and he seemed quite normal. I bent down and patted him. He growled, and our hostess said, 'Don't touch him, John. He can be a bit naughty.' I stepped back a little. Spike turned and sank two pairs of canines into my midriff. I automatically went for the scruff of his neck and tried to get him off. He released his grip, then slashed at my throat. My neck was slit open under the chin and I ended up in hospital for stitching. (This happened at the time Zimbabwe gained independence; I am reminded of the event every time I look in the mirror to shave!)

Why did Spike attack? I still do not know, but the background to the situation at that time may have had something to do with it. There was civil war in the country, and during the whole of his lifetime there were terrorists at large. Spike was a house dog, there as a deterrent. During the remainder of our short stay I had time to observe him from a safer distance. He patrolled the garden during the day and had the run of the ground floor of the house at night. That dog would give his life for his family, and any judgement of him should perhaps be tempered by remembering that he was living in troubled times.

Aggression Towards Other Dogs

A dog's aggression towards other dogs is often more difficult to control than any aggression towards people. Dominance plays such an important role in canine lives, and it is much easier to control a dog's attempted dominance over people than over other dogs. It may be our own need for dominance as pack leaders that leads so many dogs, of all breeds, to try to become the Alpha animal within its own species.

Threats of aggression against other dogs are part of the natural system of pack instinct. In the past, the German Shepherd was a development of a 'type' that was geared to the protection of sheep from predators and of the farmyard from intruders. We all know about the prowess of the German Shepherd in protecting against intruders. However, some Shepherds today seem to regard any animal from outside their own pack as a predator or a challenge to their position in the pack. Other dogs can be taken as a threat unless they are accepted as part of the dog's own community, and even within the same community there can be problems. Two very dominant dogs of the same sex within the same family circle can be a nightmare to handle.

Callum was particularly dominant and protective. If Quest had not been an old boy when Callum joined our family circle, Quest would have had to submit. No dog in his prime likes to do that, but we all have to start taking a back seat as we get older. Dogs are no different.

Callum's protectiveness could have led to problems. If he was off the lead and another dog came within his domain (which he regarded as anywhere within

Which of these is going to be the Alpha pup?

about thirty yards/metres of us), it would be fair game. He would stand four-square and look at the other dog. Usually it would turn and go away. Given half a chance, Callum would chase it out of his domain. However, he was never in a fight with another dog, partly because we were watchful and could control him, and partly because a frightened stray had good reason to run faster.

As Quest was a softer dog he was much more at ease when out walking, but there was one dog that was allowed to wander, who would cross the road rather than face him. We had just moved into a new house with three strands of wire for fencing round the garden. The dog in question belonged to a neighbour further up the street and ventured into our garden one day while Quest was sunning himself. As one would expect from any self-respecting German Shepherd, Quest gave him short shrift. When out on the street on his lead, Quest would just raise his stature enough to have this dog make a detour.

It is so easy to get into trouble when your own dog is not at fault. We had an altercation with a family while walking Isla and Duncan freely in the woods near Harrogate. I spotted a Weimaraner bitch running at us. It started barking aggressively as it closed in. I just had time to grab both dogs by the collar. The Weimaraner did not complete the attack, but circled us. At the same time the family's Jack Russell bitch joined in and launched herself at Isla's throat. The toe of my shoe sent the Jack Russell flying in the opposite direction. The owner, who had made no attempt to control his dogs, was most displeased and claimed that if I had left my dogs loose there would have been no trouble. He threatened to notify the police. I told him he was welcome to complain, but to remember that his dogs had made the attacks while mine were under full control. His bluff had been called and there was no more to be said.

On another occasion I was walking Quest, Tanya and Kerry in a country lane when a girl of about twelve, with a Labrador cross, came out of a field some thirty yards away. Her dog, which was off the lead, was well known locally for his aggression towards other dogs. The girl had absolutely no control. The dog came in fast, round behind my dogs, and latched on to the back end of Tanya. My only recourse was to use my foot, and it worked.

A few weeks later I was in a field training Kerry, still a pup. The same girl and her dog came into view. Again, the dog was free, but about fifty yards (45m) away, and it was obvious he was going to attack. This time I put Kerry on the lead, picked up a marker stick I was using, and as the dog started to charge the last ten yards or so I made a threatening counter-charge, with pup at hand, and yelled at the top of my voice. On this occasion he ran for his life.

From these and other similar situations I have learned that owners of German Shepherds tend to get the blame for any upsets which involve their dogs, whether or not they were at fault. There is another lesson. Any act of aggression on our part will only encourage a German Shepherd to be ahead of us the next time. We are in a no-win situation, and there is no doubt that, when possible, early warnings should be heeded and evasive action should be taken.

CHAPTER 6

Alertness

Of all breeds, the German Shepherd is probably considered the most watchful and alert. After all, this was one of his ancestor's principal assets, bred, as he was, to guard sheep or warn off unwanted visitors to the farm. There is a strong genetic influence here which can easily be drawn out by a dog's particular environment.

The German Shepherd's distant ancestor, the wolf (*Canis lupus*), could not survive without exceptional alertness. Finding food, particularly on the hoof, was essential for his very existence. It was the same with his defence mechanisms: he needed to ensure that predators or intruders into his domain were detected at the earliest opportunity. The defence of his pack and, with the females, the protection of the nest was crucial to the existence of the species. To maintain authority within the pack the top wolf's Alpha status also required vigilance. As the Alpha male and female were the principal breeding partners in a pack, the strength of this characteristic was consolidated from one generation to the next.

All the wolf's senses were co-ordinated to maximize his ability to detect the presence of other creatures in his vicinity. Wolves are also recognized as shy and retiring, aware of all the dangers around them. Shyness in itself will tend to create above-average alertness. Inherited genes and a harsh environment created the master of alertness in the wolf. Those qualities have not been lost throughout the many generations of breeding that have shaped our present-day German Shepherd Dog. The shyness can be witnessed in some individual members of the breed.

The Five Senses

Which of the senses are most important to the present-day German Shepherd? Only the dogs could answer that question, but hearing and smell seem to be the most highly developed and would be at the top of the list. Which of the two takes top place will depend on the individual dog and his environment at a particular time. There can be no question about the Shepherd's ability to hear well, and to use this faculty for alertness. One only has to watch the ears swivel round or the head turn to realize that the dog has picked up a sound that was not audible to a human. The ability to detect noises so easily may well put this faculty ahead of the other senses in many situations.

The alertness of the eye is not a feature of German Shepherds. Like many other breeds, they tend to be short-sighted. To spot the long-sighted animals requires the comparison of two or more dogs at a time. Most breeders and owners do not seem to

Isla with her daughter – both showing the same degree of alertness.

have given any real thought to this feature, but I have found that, for some reason, bitches are more likely to be long-sighted.

This tendency became evident with our first two dogs, Quest and Tanya. One evening when I was due home from work, Irene had come to the front gate with the two dogs to see if I was on my way. I was about 150 yards (135m) or more away when Tanya recognized me. Irene said, 'O.K., you can go and see your Dad.' Tanya was off at once, but Quest just looked, and it was some time before he realized why Tanya was running down the street.

At that time I was having problems with Tanya and her attitude towards tracking. I began to wonder if her lack of enthusiasm was connected to her long-sightedness. With this in mind, we spent time assessing the long- or short-sightedness of our dogs. There was no doubt that there was a great difference between Quest and Tanya. Callum also tended to be long-sighted and this did cause tracking problems, but in day-to-day living no distinct preference appeared to surface.

Tanya, Isla and Ceilidh all gave greater preference to the use of their ears and eyes. They were all long-sighted, and their sense of smell would only come into action when the use of their eyes was not appropriate. If they got wind of an interesting scent, they made every effort to change into viewing mode.

The effect of long-sightedness on nose-work will become more evident in Chapter 8. Suffice to say at the moment that a dog's ability to discern and recognize objects visually at a distance does have an effect on his ability and desire to apply his scenting powers. This is confirmed by the way in which gaze hounds operate. Breeds in this category have been developed to detect movement visually at a distance, and their ability to apply scenting powers cannot match that of recognized noseworking breeds.

With more than one dog in the family it is sometimes difficult to assess one against another. Duncan, Isla's son, would have to be sharp to be ahead of her and, although in his short life he was a very dominant male, his mother usually took the lead. One story illustrates Isla's vigilance and reaction ahead of Duncan. It was a Saturday morning when I took both dogs for my usual walk to collect my morning paper. This took me through a housing estate, down a fenced lane to some open ground. The dogs were kept on the lead until I reached this open ground, which was a favourite area for dog-walking and I liked to make sure there was nobody round the corner before letting my dogs free. The dogs were then put into the 'Sit' before removing the leads. As they were unclipped, Isla turned her head smartly; Duncan's head followed. I turned to see the reason. A Border Collie was charging in, with the owner just coming out of the woods some forty yards (36m) away. At this stage the Collie was about ten yards (9m) away and attacking fast. By the time I could give a hard command to 'Stay', Isla was away, with Duncan a split second behind. No dog will sit and wait to be attacked and before I had time to react they chased the Collie up the path and down the road. Although no contact was made before I got them back the other owner, an eighteen-year-old lad, had to go chasing after his dog. I had taken my usual precautions, but was caught out by a thoughtless young man. It is not always easy to be ahead of an alert German Shepherd.

At one time, we would walk the dogs in the woods every day. The path was twisty and bushes often blocked the view ahead. It was interesting to watch Caro, in particular. Whether he knew by scent or sound was difficult to tell, but he would indicate the presence of somebody, or of another dog, by his stance. His ears were as alert as antennas picking up the air waves. His nose would be trying to detect traces of scent in the air. He would stand until the source became apparent, and he was never wrong. There was always that warning stance to let us know of a 'presence'.

How important in German Shepherds are the remaining two senses? The sense of feel may not be so apparent as a factor in the dog's alertness, but it is hard to touch a Shepherd without the dog being aware of it. However minor the contact, the dog will generally register even the slightest vibration as worthy of attention. Again, circumstances will dictate the dog's reaction.

The last of the five senses is taste. Although German Shepherds must have some form of alertness as to whether objects are safe to eat, this sense does not come into our equation.

Ceilidh alert to an unusual but interesting situation.

Suspicion and Reflexes

In the German Shepherd, suspicion is a characteristic that comes with alertness. However, this should always stem from courage and not from nervousness or shyness.

A good working police dog is a shining example of a dog environmentally conditioned to the highest degree of alertness, with reflexes to match, through the medium of suspicion. With such dogs, courage and the dog's belief in his own abilities are prime factors which are encouraged throughout training.

One such reflex which sticks in my mind was the escorting exercise in the Police Dog (now known as Patrol Dog) Stake in a civilian trials. I was competing with Callum against some strong competition. This included the National Police Dog Champion of the year, W.T. Ch. Victor of Aycliffe, from Dundee City Police, handled by Jim Dykes. The 'criminal' was Jack Todd, another police dog handler who was superb in this field of training. The escort test was carried out in the manner of those days, with the competitor trailing the 'criminal' by about two paces and his dog in between. The dog's function was to protect his handler if attacked, or to prevent the 'criminal' from escaping. With such a short distance between 'criminal' and handler, this required the utmost vigilance and quick reflexes from the dog. We were caught on the hop. During this escort, Jack lifted his hand to scratch his brow – a normal thing to do on a hot day. Suddenly he grasped the peak of his

Hungry puppies will always be alert.

cap and threw it away. This was a diversion. The second Callum went for the cap, Jack turned to attack me. I shouted, 'Callum'. It was all I had time for, but his response was immediate and sure. He seemed to turn in mid-air and caught Jack beautifully on the forearm. It was a full-mark performance. (The funny sequel to this anecdote was the judge's reaction. He came to me, marking board in hand, and asked why I had shouted, 'Kill him!' I replied that I hadn't; I had just called the dog's name.) We finished in second place to the National Police Dog Champion. With these dogs, courage was an essential complement to their alertness.

Nervousness and Alertness

Unfortunately there are Shepherds that combine alertness with nervousness or shyness. These are the dogs that some breeders and owners would rather not know about. They breed them, or they own one, but rarely admit to it. Such a puppy, with good show prospects, may be kept by a breeder. He is not socialized, but the breeder can get away with that in the breed show ring. At the end of the day the early promise of success is not fulfilled, and the dog is sold on as a junior animal to a pet owner. He seemed fine at the kennels, his home environment, but uncertainty and nervousness, accompanied by acute alertness, can create 'windy aggression' of the most dangerous kind. All too often, I have received a phone call from the owner of such a youngster. It is usually after the dog has bitten somebody. It is then a long, hard haul to try and reclaim the dignity that should never have been lost in the first place.

I was attending a training class one evening and was sitting beside the club chairman who was so proud of his Shepherd. Nico was a large and quite handsome fellow, but still a junior. His eyes watched every movement and his ears seemed to be able to rotate a full turn. Alertness was the name of his game; he did not miss a thing.

At one stage, I bent down to pick up another dog's dumb-bell that had gone under my chair when Nico went for me. Fortunately the owner was as quick as the dog, and was in time to physically check him. I am sure this had happened before. He seemed unconcerned about the incident and turned to me saying what a good police dog Nico would make. I just replied, 'I would think not. He is a fear biter.'

At a later date the dog did bite, and had to be put down. If his owner had appreciated he had a problem, instead of making a virtue out of his dog's weakness, he may well have been able to counter and control the dog's unwarranted suspicion. Instead, the life of a handsome masculine Shepherd, a dear friend of his owner, had to be cut short. Nature and the environment were both against Nico.

Some puppies of sound breeding can start to show signs of drawing back into their shells if left in the breeding kennel too long. Isla was one such puppy, as I have described in Chapter 2. Fortunately, the potential problem was recognized and her breeding produced the temperament expected.

Alertness and Visitors

People coming to the house usually sharpens a German Shepherd's vigilance. There are two categories of reaction. One is to visitors known to the dog, who will be welcomed. If we say to Ceilidh, 'Is Nancy coming?', she is at the window looking for one of her favourite friends.

The same thing happens when we are in the park. Our daughter and her Shepherd use the same park. If I say, 'Is that Tegan?', Ceilidh is all eyes and ears, scanning the park for her best four-legged friend.

We could call the second type of visit detached or incomplete. These are visits from people who come to the door, usually leave something, and go away – for example the milk boy and the postman. They come to the front door, the dog hears them and barks. They are at the door for a second or two, then turn and go away. The dog thinks he is responsible for getting rid of this uninvited visitor. The next time he is more alert and waiting; he has nothing else to do. At the first indication of such a visitor, he is there barking. He again has success: the visitor has, he thinks, been chased away. His alertness and reactions are now very predictable; but they can be dangerous. Polly's fate was in the balance because of just such an event.

Polly's owner was in court, charged with owning a dangerous dog. Polly had bitten the milk boy, who had been standing at the front door being paid. There was no question, no doubt, and no aggravation from the boy. This was an unprovoked attack. The owners did not believe Polly was a bad dog, in fact she was great with the children. They were prepared to plead guilty but did not want to lose their dog. I was called in by their solicitor to do a character assessment and try to defend Polly.

I visited the house and, although Polly barked and was on the lead when we were introduced at the door, I had no problem in entering the house after we had accepted each other.

The background to this lovely natured dog began to unfold. She was four years old and had been with the family for

A puppy alert to the promise of a juicy reward.

about six months. Her earlier life was the problem. She had been taken on as a young puppy by an elderly couple. A path that ran along the top of their garden led to the school, and Polly was teased by the children going to and from school. This became too much of a problem for the elderly couple, and she was given to a builder's merchant to guard their premises at night.

She was eventually considered to be too friendly with the customers to make a good guard dog, and she was passed on again, to the family in question, as a pet-cum-warning dog. She settled in well, had the run of the house, and became the home protector. She barked at all the 'incomplete visits': by the milk boy, the postman, and anybody else who dared to come and go. She was always shut in the kitchen when the door was opened to a visitor, and on the day she bit the milk

boy it had been no different. Unfortunately, however, one of the children opened the kitchen door. Polly was through it like a shot, down the hall, and catching the unsuspecting boy before he could move.

In court, the solicitor for the dog's defence was recognizing the failure to control the dog but was pleading for her life. As an expert witness, I gave a summary of Polly's background and the situation that had developed regarding 'incomplete visits'.

The magistrates' verdict was one that could not have been delivered anywhere in the UK but in Scotland: the 'dangerous dog' charge was found 'not proven'. The owners had learned quite a lesson, and on my advice Polly was not allowed the run of the house at the times of these 'incomplete visits'. She was never in trouble again.

Laid-Back Alertness

When our dogs are left in the car, they may, at times, appear to be asleep – but I always feel that my car is much safer with them in the back. German Shepherds always seem to be alert, even when they appear to be sleeping or dozing. They may well sleep through many normal events that are part of their daily life. Doors opening and closing when members of the family go out and in may be ignored by a resting Shepherd. However, any slight change in the pattern of events – perhaps when a coat is taken off the peg – will prompt him to be up and ready with that look that says, 'What about me? You can't leave me behind.'

Alertness in a German Shepherd often seems to be combined with an outwardly relaxed attitude. A hotel guard dog was probably the best example I have seen. Aldo was an ageing, large, over-fed, laid-back lump of a German Shepherd. He would lie in the entrance hall, and all who entered would have to walk round him. Aldo had no intention of moving for anybody. He was not there to guard during office hours; that would have scared clients away. He was there for night-time. When the doors were locked for the night, Aldo took over. If any movement on the ground floor was detected, everybody knew about it. The drinks in the bar and the valuables in the office were safe with Aldo around. His perception of situations and his lifetime of learning had made him the most effective laid-back guard in the business.

CHAPTER 7

Resilience

The resilience that the German Shepherd has inherited from his ancestor, the wolf, may not seem to be important to the pet dog owner, but the residual effects of this characteristic can make a difference to a dog's life span. The ability to cope with illness is clearly a great asset. German Shepherds with a job of work to do will also show the value of resilience in many different ways.

What is Resilience?

The factors that together make up the quality of resilience contribute to the dog's overall strength of the German Shepherd's character. The resilient dog will have:

- The capacity to bear discomfort.
- Toughness and staying power.
- The ability to concentrate for lengthy periods.
- Grit and endurance.
- The ability to take a knock and come back again
- Bounce and buoyancy.
- Good physical and mental recuperative powers.

The physical and mental resources that a dog has inherited through his genes may well take time to develop, but like other genetic factors they can be consolidated through careful management – or can be destroyed by an unsuitable environment.

German Shepherds today are the result of the integrated breeding of dogs that were used to herd and protect sheep. This task required endurance, toughness, and the capacity to sustain hours of tireless activity. The clearly visible legacy to the Shepherds of our time is the measure of resilience that is the hallmark of the breed.

Endurance is of the greatest importance in dogs that have to work for their keep. In most countries today, German Shepherds are employed by the various services. Protection and nosework account for most of their activities, and both can be very demanding. Police dog handlers, in particular, have many tales to tell about their dogs' ability to accept setbacks but to keep on going. Human lives depend on these working dogs being resilient under adverse conditions.

Developing Resilience

Good handlers understand the need to develop the German Shepherd's natural resilience by providing a stimulating environment. Teaching a young dog to cope with situations that require toughness – the ability to take a knock and come back again – is achieved by steadily building up his confidence. This is done by enabling him to experience major successes, and to overcome minor discomforts that become gradually more severe as he progresses. This requires a considerate handler and a team of helpers who have the expertise to create the challenges that will enhance the Shepherd's inherited strength of character. On the other hand, there are instances in which young dogs have been broken by inconsiderate handling. These dogs lose their capacity to react with strength to situations that should be within the scope of their expected ability to bounce back.

I recall one young Shepherd many years ago. He was known as Ludi, and came from top-class breeding. Unfortunately he was overshadowed in the show ring by a litter-sister, Laura, who became a breed champion. The breeder offered him to the police. Ludi was a grandson of our old P.D. Champion Quest. He had Quest's gentleness about him, was without vices, and had been brought up to experience life outside the confines of the kennels. He was a well-adjusted youngster before his introduction to a police environment. What happened during that short spell away from his home we do not know, but he was returned to the breeder a few days later as unsatisfactory for the rigours of professional duties.

It seemed that this youngster had been given no time to settle in before he was assessed. The assessment may have been rough; an attempt to induce aggression may have been crudely carried out. The activities during those few days were enough to break his spirit. Afterwards, Ludi found strangers and unusual situations very difficult to accept. He never left home again. I think that if Quest, his grandsire, had been subjected to a similar situation as a junior, he too would have folded under the stress of such a dramatic change in his way of life.

I doubt whether such a situation would be allowed to develop today, but it clearly shows how a young dog's life can be ruined by an insensitive introduction to protection training, and just how easy it is to shatter the future of a promising youngster. Quest, and many Shepherds like him, have become much better dogs, with much greater resilience, through their involvement in protection work. They have revelled in it, and learned to take knocks and eagerly come back for more; but they have achieved this only through gradual and intelligent handling.

Determination

Determination is at the root of resilience and that determination can show itself in many different ways. It may be very strong in one field and very weak in another. It is acknowledged that in some breeding lines, nosework with the tenacity to follow a cold track for a lengthy period is very strong; but the desire to become involved in protection work is much weaker. With other Shepherds, the natural tenacity to go in for the bite, to hold on under very difficult circumstances, is unbelievably strong, yet many of these same dogs are likely to lack the inherited drive for tracking. Under these circumstances it takes ingenuity and hard work to counter the shortfall in the appropriate genes and create an enjoyable experience for the dog.

Two of my own dogs illustrate this point. Although Quest won his tickets in P.D. to become a champion, his natural

Determination to outdo his litter-mate.

ability had a very strong leaning towards nosework. Both he and I got more pleasure out of tracking, yet our greatest successes came from protection work. Callum was the complete opposite. He was a 'macho' dog, born for protection work. It came so naturally to him. He had the capacity to take shock treatment and come back for more. He had the toughness and staying power to hold on. This was already evident when he was about a year old and Quest was a very fit ten-year-old. Quest, still young at heart, had found an old jute sack. Callum wanted it, and got hold of the other end. This was the beginning of a lengthy tug-of-war. Quest had to give ground from the start, and finally gave up. Callum pranced around with his trophy; although he was quite obedient I had a problem taking the sack from him: his jaws were locked and it took time to unlock them.

There was a similar situation about two years later when Callum was mature and was entered in a club rally with pro-tection work on the agenda. One test involved a 'criminal' padded up in a small room with a big 45 revolver (firing blanks). The judges were watching through the window when the dog was sent in to disarm the 'criminal'. A single shot would be fired when the dog was in the room with the door closed. The judges were to assess the dog's reaction to the shot. With Callum, the shot was fired and I entered the room to find the 'criminal' completely immobilized, the gun dangling from his trigger finger and Callum firmly latched on to the padded arm. The man was in agony from the pressure through the padding. After that Callum became known as 'the bone cruncher'. But, for all his natural drive for protection work, I had to find the key that would unlock his much more elusive tracking instincts.

On a much simpler level, Shepherds can differ in their ability to maintain a level of concentration or endurance. This can be affected by maturity and the real-ization of enjoyment from encourage-

A test of strength and resilience.

ment. For example, Caro was a natural carrier: a stick, a tin can, anything that took his fancy. This possessiveness, this determination to carry, was apparent by the time he was five months old and became the cornerstone of our approach in training.

Ceilidh was the opposite. She would pick up something we had thrown, or something she had found, walk a few paces, drop it, and then carry on without it. She became known as 'pea-brain' or 'butterfly-mind'. Her span of concentration during those first few months of her life was as short as it could possibly be. This was a feature of Ceilidh's general attitude unless the subject really interested her. From the little bits and pieces we did, protection work could have become the centre of her life and the stimulant for other things. Unfortunately my own lack of fitness prevented this activity. It took time and much encouragement to build up in Ceilidh a positive attitude towards carrying. She is now possessive over her throw toys, and will carry them for evermore.

However, if resilience includes 'stubbornness', Ceilidh came into the world with her whole litter's quota and more.

If any of these dogs had gone as puppies into pet homes, without a thought of training, these differences may never have been noticed.

Resilience and Ill-Health

The concept of endurance is much more meaningful with German Shepherds that have to work for their keep. In many countries, including the UK, Shepherds are often employed by the Services, and protection and nosework will make up a large proportion of their activities.

As we have said, protection work demands a great deal of physical effort. It was the preparation for the civilian P.D. Stake that highlighted Callum's lack of physical endurance. We were out training for the protection side of the test when it became apparent that he was beginning to lose steam on the quarter and search. Jim Dykes, the Dundee police dog sergeant who was acting 'criminal', said, 'That dog's not fit.'

I had to agree with him. Although Callum had the drive, or mental capacity,

Ceilidh became a dedicated carrier.

revealed nothing, it was decided to take him to Glasgow Veterinary College for X-rays. (This was many years before hip X-rays became standard practice.) One hip was normal but, as I have already mentioned in Chapter 5, the other was very bad indeed. I have seen many X-ray plates since, but none as bad as this one.

After leaving the college, I drove for a few miles, found a lay-by, stopped, and wept. A dog who had given me so much in the first two-and-a-half years of his life, including the work we both enjoyed so much, was coming to the end of his career.

When the report from the college came through, I discussed the situation with Mr Thomson, a good and understanding vet. I was all for calling a halt, but it was only weeks away from the Scottish Championship P.D. event and he said, 'A little longer won't do him any harm. We can give him a course of cortisone to see him through.'

Callum did us proud. He gained his qualification, and second place. He was rested for a year, then entered for the T.D. Championship event where he gained the trophy for the best track and search. He could no longer jump, however, and did not qualify. Although Callum's working career was over, we did carry on with some Obedience competitions. Once a German Shepherd's mind has been stimulated, he wants to work.

The evidence of Callum's resilience to pain did not stop there, and it seems appropriate to relate the episode that resulted in a better life for him. The condition of his hip was deteriorating; occasionally the head of the femur would come out of its socket and he would fall over. His life was going to be cut short. However, our luck changed. It all started with a phone call from Jack Livey,

to carry on, physically he was slowing down. During the next few weeks I borrowed my daughter's bicycle to bring Callum up to fitness with road work. As it turned out, it was the worst thing I could have done. Initially he was keen to come out but, in due course, he started to lag behind. At the same time a badly set up scale-jump collapsed under him. Again, my fault for not checking it first.

He was rested, but the situation did not improve and I took him to the vet for examination, asking if he should have his hips X-rayed. The vet replied that Callum had gone through the trials without problems so far, and had been jumping O.K. He doubted whether his hips were to blame. After a fuller examination, which

An indication of Callum's jumping ability before the effects of a hip dysplasia finished his working career.

Inspector in charge of the Strathclyde Police Dog Section.

My misfortune with Callum was well known throughout the trials fraternity, and this included the many police dog sections that were involved in the trialling scene. It was appreciated that I would not part with him, but nevertheless I was aware that I had a dog that was now three years old and no longer able to compete, which was deeply disappointing. My role for the foreseeable future would be that of instructing others and helping at trials.

Inspector Livey had much contact with the Glasgow Veterinary College and the renowned hip specialist, Professor Lawson, who had carried out operations on smaller pet dogs to counter the effects of hip dysplasia. Briefly, this involved the removal of the head of the femur to alleviate the pain caused by the grating of bone to bone and the other related prob-

lems. Professor Lawson wanted to see if a working dog could benefit from this operation. A lot of time and money goes into training a police dog, and this operation could help such a dog to continue with his active service.

Since Strathclyde had no appropriate dogs at that time, Inspector Livey suggested Callum as a candidate. As he had already been X-rayed at the college, they already knew of him and had his records. With our own vet's co-operation, an appointment was made and we had a full and frank discussion with Professor Lawson about the implications. Although the possibilities looked promising, the bottom line, according to Professor Lawson, was that Callum would be better off without the head of the femur in that socket.

It was suggested that we take time to think about it. We were not put under any pressure. We had travelled about ninety miles (145km) to the college. I asked when the operation could be done, if we agreed. 'Tomorrow, if you wanted.'

Irene and I went for a walk in the grounds to discuss the situation. It was quite an operation. Our thoughts were not on whether Callum could go back to competitive work, but on his shortened life span if we turned our backs on this opportunity. He was a big, heavy dog: we often said that he was built like an Aberdeen Angus bull.

Rather than take him home and come back at a later date we decided to leave him for the operation.

Unfortunately, the femur broke when the head was being removed, and had to be pinned back in place. The socket was now without the ball joint, scar tissue was created as a cushion, and the ligaments were tightened to give the best alternative to the one designed by nature. We have known of dogs that did not have the mental resilience to cope with the trauma of such an operation, but Callum took it in his stride.

After the operation, we had to make regular return visits to the veterinary college so that Callum's progress could be checked and assessed. During two of these visits he had been lifted up on to the X-ray table. On the third occasion, he knew what was coming, and before anyone could pick him up he turned tail and started to walk out of the room. I called, 'Come on son, you are going up whether you like it or not.' He turned towards me, and then suddenly leapt from the floor and landed squarely on top of the table with a look that said, 'If I am going up, I'll do it my way.' The veterinary staff looked on in amazement.

I was told that in a little more time he could try and return to agility training. Eventually Callum could make five feet six inches (168cm) on the scale-jump – six

inches (15cm) short of the competition height. And he could do seven feet (84cm) on the long jump, which was two feet (61cm) short of the requirements. The strength of his fore-shoulders allowed him to pull himself over the scale-jump, but he could not get the stretch in his hindquarters for long jump. The three-foot (90cm) clear jump was also a problem. Again it was the hindquarters that had to do all the work. The clear jump problem came to the fore when we were out for a country walk one day. We came to a low wire-netting fence. Jeza jumped it with great relish; Callum looked at it and just charged. He made no attempt to take off, but with head down he tried to go through it. I think there really must have been a bit of Aberdeen Angus bull about him.

Callum had a grand life and gave us ten years of pleasure before his other hip joint, which had taken the load for so many years, finally gave way. However, that operation had extended his life and made it a memorable one in so many ways.

There are times when one disaster follows another. As I have already mentioned in Chapter 3, about a week after the loss of Callum, Jeza almost followed. Although her temperament was good, and this quiet, good-natured soul made a lovely pet, she did not have great strength of character. This was partly through her breeding, but Callum was also responsible. As a six-month-old pup coming into our home, after being shunted from pillar to post, Jeza took Callum to be her new anchor. She adored and idolized him. He had been missing from her life for a week and we think she knew he was not coming back. She became very ill, passing blood at both ends. It was haemorrhagic enteritis. The vet was not too hopeful but gave us medication to be given hourly for the

Caro's determination was the root of his resilience.

next twenty-four hours. We slept with her in the lounge and dosed her as prescribed. It was the same again, every two hours, the next night. She pulled through. We felt that the most probable cause of her problem was stress, caused by the loss of Callum. Fortunately, Jeza's basic will to live, her resilience and our dedication turned the tide.

She was on her own with us for about six months before Caro came into our lives as a fifteen-week youngster. Jeza had already changed. She was more self-reliant and, initially, she was not going to accept this squirt of a substitute for old Callum. For three days she ignored him

completely. He wanted to play but she brushed off his advances until she realized that he was here to stay. She then took up the role of her predecessors and would shepherd him in. While walking the fields, Caro would lag behind with a stick in his mouth. She would get worried and go back for him, and showed her annoyance if he ignored her attentions. In time Caro became quite the 'macho' dog, but when the chips were down Jeza was the boss.

It is said that lightning does not strike twice in the same place. We felt that Jeza's bout of haemorrhagic enteritis had been more than our share of a potentially fatal illness that could test the resilience of young dogs. To lose an older dog is upsetting but inevitable; but the thought of losing any canine companion in their prime is never on one's mind until the probability stares you in the face.

Duncan was just seventeen months old when haemorrhagic enteritis re-entered our lives. This affliction always appears when it is least expected. Although he had appeared a bit down, there was no warning in Duncan's case, and no stressful situation to trigger the illness. The vet was mystified. There was just no apparent reason for this attack on an otherwise healthy youngster.

We were staying with our daughter in Colchester at the time. I had spent most of the week judging the Championship T.D. Stake at the Iceni GSD Club Working Trials, and it was Saturday evening. There was one day to go: the Control and Agility was to be worked on the Sunday. The dogs were fed in the early evening, but Duncan did not seem to be his usual bouncy self. He eventually finished his meal, probably to prevent the other dogs from claiming anything that was left.

We were a little concerned about Duncan, but there was nothing we could put a finger on. We were going out to the club function as guests and took Duncan in the car with us. I popped out in the middle of the evening to check on him and he seemed to be sleeping off his problems; however, we decided to leave early to get him home. Besides, the next day would be long and tiring: the final day of judging, with a lot of dogs to get through.

Duncan and his mother, Isla, both slept in the bedroom with us and this was very fortunate. At three in the morning Duncan's inside erupted. Everything passed through his bowels and it was saturated with blood. We had never smelt anything like it.

Colin, our son-in-law, took over. Being a police dog handler he had a very good relationship with his local vet. He phoned, explained the situation, and was instructed to get Duncan down to the surgery straight away. We arrived at the same time as the vet, and Duncan was in the right hands within half an hour.

He was in a very poor way. We patiently watched and waited as he was being examined. I could feel the worst of premonitions coming over me and asked the vet if I was going to lose him. He looked up and said, 'I don't know, but we will do our best for him.' That told us how serious the situation was. We left him at the surgery, having been instructed to phone about ten in the morning for an update.

There was no more sleep for us that night, and we discussed the trials the following day and how to handle it. We could do no more to help Duncan and, as we all had jobs to do at the trials, we would carry on as planned. Colin would phone the surgery at the appropriate time.

The news soon circulated round the trials and my competitors were very understanding. In particular, Joan Milne, a retired vet and a fellow competitor of many years' standing, was very concerned. She asked all the right questions, then said, 'I hope that vet knows what he is doing; if not you are going to lose Duncan.' Since Jeza's day, science had moved on and there were now more up-to-date approaches to countering this problem, and Joan hoped that this vet's approach and procedure was up with the times.

Joan was there when Colin came back with an update on Duncan's condition. 'The vet says he is improving and to phone back

The ill-fated Duncan. So much to give; so little time to give it.

at five tonight.' Joan's immediate reaction was, 'He'll come through now, and will be much better within the next twenty-four hours.' Joan could not have been more positive, and we were grateful for her confidence. My mind was now at rest and I could get on with my work for the day.

Joan was right, and when we phoned the surgery we were told that we could take Duncan home. The vet thought that would be better than leaving him alone in the surgery all night, and asked to see him again the next morning. Although Duncan was still very weak, with the vet's approval we were able to drive home a few days later. It was a ten-hour journey, but as Duncan was a good traveller the vet thought it would be restful. At home, our own vet observed Duncan's recovery and recommended a Hills diet.

Duncan's natural resilience had helped him pull him through although, tragically, he was to succumb to a severe kidney infection two years later (*see* Chapter 10).

CHAPTER 8

Agility and Suppleness

There is no question that the German Shepherd is expected to be agile, but the various authorized breed standards are short on requirements. The German Standard states that he should have 'a long-reaching tireless trotting gait' and the tireless action of a working dog. The British Standard says he should be 'capable of endurance and speed and of quick and sudden movement'.

These physical characteristics are important to the breed but unfortunately they are based on a requirement that is outdated for most of today's dogs. This requirement is for sheep herding and is quite inadequate for some of the tasks being carried out by many of today's working German Shepherds. For example, the breed standards contain no reference to the dogs' agility, as seen in their ability to jump.

Jumping Ability

The ability to clear or scramble over obstacles is one of the basic requirements for today's working German Shepherds. Whether in the police, the armed services or the civilian competitive field, all dogs must have the ability and fitness to jump. They can have fences to clear, brooks or ditches to negotiate or walls to scramble over. With these requirements in mind,

various tests have been devised within the services and civilian organizations for assessing abilities in that field after the appropriate training. The Kennel Club requirements in Working Trials give good guidance on the nature of assessments on canine agility. The three types of equipment and their sizes which cover German Shepherds are as follows:

1. Clear jump. An obstacle three feet (90cm) high to be cleared.
2. Long jump. An obstacle nine feet (2.75m) long to be cleared.
3. Scale-jump. An obstacle six feet (1.8m) high to be scrambled.

I have heard it said on a number of occasions and by top breeder/exhibitors in this country that, in order to have the ability to jump, our dogs must be constructed as near to the standard as possible. Yet the breed standards from the various countries give no indication of 'agility' and, although fitness in itself is important, the prime conception of being 'agile' is for the purpose of movement and gaiting for lengthy periods of time. They should have 'a long-reaching tireless trotting gait'. It is also well recognized within the breed fraternity that their best dogs go into the show ring and many a 'substandard' dog is sold off to the services or to Working Trials enthusiasts as a working dog.

Tackling the six-foot (1.8m) scale-jump.

I do not believe that the construction of the dog to the standard is vitally important for jumping. Fitness is of greater importance. From my own observations over many years of training and judging Working Trials, any Shepherd that is fit, co-ordinated and 'properly' trained will be as successful as its counterpart that meets every inch of the standard. Breeders and/or exhibitors have always put such importance on the hind angulation of our dogs, and have no doubt justified this by the requirement for a 'tireless trotting gait'. However, when I compare the construction of the Dobermann with that of the German Shepherd, there is no doubt that the tremendous jumping capabilities of that breed are streets ahead of those of our Shepherds. I am not criticizing the breed, the breeders, or the standard, but it is my belief that approaching the standard in perfection does not improve a dog's ability to jump. I hope this helps to put the subject into its proper perspective.

Teenage brother and sister training their German Shepherds on the nine-foot (2.75m) long jump (above) and three-foot (90cm) clear jumps.

I recall, years ago, a Working Trials fun rally held in Scotland on the estate of the late Miss Moncrieffe. It included a long jump competition. This started with the regulation nine feet and, as the jump was lengthened, the various dogs were knocked out until there was one left. The organizers kept lengthening the jump until the dog failed, but the winner – a Shepherd that would never have graced the show ring – cleared an amazing eighteen feet.

Some Shepherds are naturals for jumping. Quest found it to be a most enjoyable activity and was in competition at the time of the retrieve over the six-foot scale. Kerry, his daughter, inherited more than her share of her sire's genes. She would tackle anything at any time. Point to a wall and she would be over in a flash. (We always had to check the other side before asking her to jump.) She was so sure-footed and it was the only area where she was naturally confident. A fallen tree inclined at an angle was no problem; she could run up, turn, and run down again. As mentioned earlier, we gifted Kerry to the R.A.F. and she became the star of their demonstration team, on one occasion performing the tightrope walk at the Royal Tournament in London. It was a proud night when we sat and watched.

Jeza, our other bitch who was softer in character, did the unthinkable in training. It usually takes a great deal of time for a dog to build up in height on the scale-jump, in particular. Most dogs take months of careful step-by-step increases of two to three inches (5–8cm) at a time, with periods of consolidation in between. Jeza graduated from about three feet (90cm) to the full six feet (1.8m) in one afternoon. A good solid foundation had been put into the earlier stages of her

training, and the rest was easy. She was an exception, and this is not an approach I would normally recommend.

Ceilidh was not the best of jumpers, and initially there seemed to be no good reason for this. Her hips were good, she was fit, and yet I could not generate the enthusiasm to make her keen on agility. She could and did jump, but found the full height of the scale-jump to be a struggle. Ceilidh had one fall from the scale-jump, and it took a little while to generate sufficient interest to rebuild her confidence.

As I have mentioned, Ceilidh did have hormone problems through her early years. Initially this was not fully appreciated, but we eventually realized that there was an identity problem. At the same time my own mobility was very much in question. This may have had an effect on my own enthusiasm and ability to help Ceilidh. As I had to retire from the practical side of training before Ceilidh reached her prime and overcame her problems, it would not be fair to opt out of all responsibility. The fact was that, when out walking free, Ceilidh would enjoy jumping on to or over fallen trees.

Quest, Caro and Callum all enjoyed training for the jumps. Training was taken nice and easily, with the rewards of success. Callum took it in his stride, even with a very bad hip, until it got too much for him. He would never have given up; he was a trier.

Duncan was different. He was a big dog, well above the standard. In height he was nearer to a Great Dane than a German Shepherd. He was our own breeding and I was embarrassed by his size and refused to have him measured. He must have been about twenty-nine inches (73cm) to the shoulder. One would have expected him to be a good candidate for Working

Suppleness counts in the weaving exercise in Agility tests.

Trials Agility. Alas, it was not to be. He could cope with the scale-jump, but it was a struggle. He could manage the clear jump, but not as easily as one would expect. The long jump was frustrating. He enjoyed it, but rarely cleared the nine feet (2.75m). He had size, he had limitless energy, he could stretch his movement in a gallop when in play but, try as he might, he rarely managed the long jump.

Our daughter, Frances, was watching one day and came up with the explanation for his inability. Apart from being very involved in dog training, she is a swimming instructor and spends much of her time teaching young children. 'That dog is not co-ordinated,' she said, then continued, 'I have seen this often in children. They cannot co-ordinate arms and legs.'

She had spotted the cause of the problem right away. But, although we could now see the reason for the problem, we would not have time to find the solution, for we lost Duncan at the age of three years. But that is another story.

Speed

'Capable of speed and of quick and sudden movement' is part of the U.K. Breed Standard and this is of vital importance to working police dogs. They must be very agile. We do not normally have the opportunity of seeing those dogs in action unless they are involved in demonstrations or competitions, but in the field of competitive Working Trials we can watch or take

In pursuit of a criminal, speed, suppleness and power are combined in Tegan's movement, from the stretch forward ...

part. The speed that some Shepherds can attain, and their ability to turn and change direction, is a pleasure to see. Our younger daughter, Joyce, has a Shepherd bitch of top-quality breeding, but it is doubtful if Tegan's construction would bring honours in the show ring. However, her speed and length of stride are just out of this world. I doubt if I have ever seen a faster Shepherd in action. The ability to use such speed, to turn and latch on to a 'criminal' brings together many of the attributes that makes the breed ideal for this work.

Gait

'A long-reaching tireless trotting gait' comes from the German Standard and this is an important characteristic for a tracking dog. It is not perhaps essential for the dog in civilian competitions, where the dog is tracking for a period of ten to twenty minutes, but police dogs are often asked to track for much longer periods.

It may be an old cliché, but to watch a well-constructed Shepherd tracking is 'poetry in motion'. One of my greatest pleasures has always been to admire the concentration and movement in action. Although I could watch and admire my own dogs from the rear I did not have the opportunity to observe the actions of my earlier dogs from the side. It was only the introduction of video recorders that gave me that privilege. I have watched many a Shepherd gait round the show ring. However, I feel that the true movement of the breed is captured at its best when a dog is pulling into the harness; nose down and legs propelling his body with that effortless gait.

There is an interesting anecdote relating to Caro, who was probably the best-bred dog I have owned and worked. Both Caro and I loved to go out tracking and

... to the preparation for the next stride.

when Caro tracked it was on the end of a very tight line. He was a powerful dog and even on a long track in deep heather he could pull his exhausted handler up the hillside. At the end of the track I would lie down to get my breath back. Caro was still very fresh and could have gone on.

At the time of the event in question he had qualified T.D.Ex. in Working Trials and was also 'V' rated in the breed ring – a very rare combination. He was being exhibited in the Open class at an Open GSD breed show under a recognized breed judge. After the individual assessments, the dogs were placed with Caro in second or third position. His chances of a place card looked good, but as they were moved round and round and round for an interminable period of time, Caro slipped back in the line. At the completion of the judge's deliberation he was 'tail-end Charlie'. This was a new experience for us, but it was obvious this judge was con-

scious of one aspect of movement only. The dogs that pulled hard on the lead and showed mindless drive round the ring were looked on with favour.

It was true that we had lost a place or two in the past because Caro did not show the drive in the ring that he put into tracking; but never to this extent. The judge, breaking Kennel Club regulations, decided to give a verbal and public critique on each dog in the class. He pronounced that Caro could have finished much higher up, but that he did not have the stamina for a lengthy gaiting session. Caro was well known to most of the exhibitors there, and this judge could not have made a bigger mistake. He could not differentiate between a fit, well-muscled working dog that was bored out of his mind and an unfit specimen.

It is a pity we have to rely on the artificial conditions of the breed ring to assess our Shepherds against the Standard.

CHAPTER 9

Scenting Ability

A German Shepherd's scenting ability is so enormous in comparison with that of man that it is difficult to grasp the magnitude of the difference. We can read about it, write about it, work with it and study it; but the scenting ability of dogs is still a mystery. To the dog, the use of his nose to follow scents and discriminate between them is second nature. It is the most natural activity in the world. The problem is a human one – of understanding how and why the various scents take his interest.

Our knowledge on this subject is based on practical experience and theoretical deductions from the German Shepherd's abilities. This is a subject for a book in its own right and here I can only give a brief insight into a very fascinating topic.

Scenting Work

In order to understand and visualize what the German Shepherd can do, it is perhaps useful to give some background to the scenting activities they may be asked to perform.

The most common is tracking – following the human scent left on the ground by a person walking. This could be a criminal at the scene of a crime, or it could be a missing person. Searching for lost or hidden articles is another task and, although searching buildings or yards for

a hidden criminal may seem to come into the same category, the training is completely different.

Scent discrimination – distinguishing between the body scent of one person and that of another – is principally used in Obedience competition, and is gaining greater credibility in police work throughout Europe. Many dogs are also trained to detect the presence of a single substance by its unique odour. Drugs and explosives are obvious examples. One expert, by the name of Glen Johnson, in Canada, trained his Shepherd to detect leaks in natural-gas pipelines. His success rate was believed to be better than that of the appropriate man-made apparatus for the job.

Some of these activities are widely used by civilian dog-owners in various fields of competition. They give a very interesting outlet for the owners of all breeds, but this is an area where German Shepherds do tend to excel.

Scenting Theories

Some of the ideas in this section come with substantial backing from the experience of many people, but quite a lot come from logical thinking. Trial and error has enabled me to whittle many theories down to a few. I have found my own approach to illustrating the theories which I believe to be the soundest. These theories have helped me lay the foundation for sound nosework performances. Much of what appears here was first published some twenty years ago in my book *Nosework for Dogs* and included in the Crowood edition of *Training the German Shepherd Dog* (see Further Reading). However, I feel some of it is worth repeating.

As humans, we find it difficult to recognize the presence of more than one scent at a time. To us, one strong scent will mask all others. When new-mown grass is present, we cannot smell anything else. When bacon is being fried, no other scents seem to exist. The most dominant scent at any one time captivates our whole olfactory system. Dogs, on the other hand, can pick and choose between the scents and odours they wish to concentrate on. They can ignore any dominant scent that is around and concentrate on some minor scent that has taken their attention. A dog can track through a field recently spread with farmyard manure that can turn the stomach of his handler. He can maintain his intense attention on the much fainter odour created by the track-layer.

A dog's appreciation of scents has certain similarities with our own powers of vision. We can see any number of objects at one time. We can focus on one item and follow its course, and at the same time we can visually monitor surrounding objects and detect their presence. We can direct our focus on to any of the other items at will, yet still be aware of all other objects within our range of vision.

A dog tracking can be compared to a human driving a car. As we drive, we concentrate on the road ahead. We can focus on anything that may affect our direction or speed in order to take appropriate action. Our peripheral and unfocused forward or side vision helps guide us along the correct part of the road. Dogs have the same ability with scent focusing. They can be well aware of the many scents and odours in the atmosphere, ignore the most dominant if they wish, and give their full attention to any of the subordinate scents that leads them to their objective. However, they will still be aware of all the scents in the area. They can bypass a dominant odour because of the significance of some minor scent. This canine ability to focus on a single subordinate scent or combination of scents is a distinctive attribute which has never been matched by any instrument or machine.

Types of Scent

The various scents that are generally mixed in the atmosphere can be broken down into three basic types: animal scents, ground odours and material odours.

Animal scents require consideration, principally the scent from human beings. Once a dog has picked up the scent path created by a human, he is expected to maintain contact with that scent and ignore the scent of any other human being who has ventured into the area. This can take us back to the wolf following an injured animal. He is mentally focused on this particular beast. Another animal crosses its path and, unless he thinks this is a more likely meal ticket, he will maintain contact with his original choice. We use the same principle with a tracker dog.

Other animal scents also play their part. The wolf's principal objectives were of the four-legged variety, just as an untrained dog will get his greatest pleasure from following the scent of another animal that interests him. It may be

Caro discriminates between the scents in the cloths ...

another dog, a cat, a rabbit or even a bird that has been grounded. The scent may be strongest on the ground or it may be airborne. These animal scents, which are so enticing and interesting, cause problems to the trained tracking dog. They give rise to a conflict of interest – pleasure against work. It is only when we make purposeful tracking a greater pleasure that we can have dogs ignore the disruptive and distracting scents.

This brings in the difference between the scent from one person and that from another. In tracking, we do not want a dog to change from the scent left by one person to that of another which may be fresher and easier to follow. In scent discrimination it can be a highly skilled process to have a dog maintain his interest in the scent from one person against a collection of others. For him to distinguish between one person and another there must be a difference in the scent that comes from each individual. Every person carries a distinctive scent of his own which is conveyed through perspiration via the moisture in the air. It may be that there are more general distinctions, say between men and women, or between people of different ethnic origins. It could be that there are similarities among people who share the same blood group or other physiological feature. At the moment there does not seem to be any way for us to classify such scents and we are fully dependent on our dogs to identify a person by the scent that comes from the body. To the dog, this scent is a form of fingerprint but he recognizes it more readily than a policeman searching records. Dogs can differentiate between one scent and another in an instant. However, although any self-respecting dog can discriminate, it takes a specially trained dog to inform us of his selection by scent.

Ground odours are of great value to the tracking dog. When a dog is following a

... and presents the correct one.

particular human scent, there will be many other scents or odours in the atmosphere. Some are of no value but others, such as the odours from disturbed soil or bruised vegetation, may well be of more help to the dog than the human scent itself. For example, the dog may follow the odour caused by bruised vegetation but keep in mind that it was created by the presence of a particular human being. Some dogs can track just as well on a ploughed field as they can on pasture, provided the time delay is not too long.

Material odours cannot be discounted on a track. The scent from footwear will be left on the ground. The bottoms of trousers will leave a certain amount of scent on the undergrowth as the track-layer passes by. Every material has its own scent. We tend to think of plastics as

being all the same, but different plastics give off different odours. I have brought this subject up with experts in the field of polymers and they have looked very vague. We seem to know so little about the scents of materials, but experience has told me that dogs can detect some plastics more easily than others.

One example involved Caro. I was working in a factory manufacturing electrical wires and cables at the time, and was able to get lengths of scrap P.V.C. cable jacket to use as articles for retrieves, or search and track articles. They were usually cut into lengths of about six inches (15cm) and there were always a few in the car for use at any time. We had hitched up the caravan for a long autumn weekend at a quiet site by Loch Rannoch. When we arrived on the site and were starting to set up camp, we let the dogs free. They never strayed. Caro started rummaging in a large bed of ferns beside the caravan and came out with a piece of P.V.C. jacketing. It had been there since our previous visit a year earlier. There would be no human or doggy scent left on it, but Caro knew the scent of this particular plastic.

Caro was also mad about golf balls. We lived by a golf course, and during our daily walks on the course he would spend his time searching in the rough for balls. During one half-hour walk he found nineteen golf balls. He became known to some of the golfers and we were happy to help a player search for a lost ball. Caro would never touch a ball on the fairway and became the golfers' friend.

During my earliest days of dogging I also played golf. I was not a good golfer, but Quest was often my saviour. He would keep me company on most outings, and after I played a shot he could pick up the scent of the ball as it bounced on the fairway. He would then follow the 'run' of the ball. While it was on the fairway we could see the ball but Quest would use his nose to trace the 'run' to its final resting place. If the ball was hit straight into the rough he would still find it. There was plenty of practice for him and he did nothing for the quality of my play.

During this period Quest was an Obedience and Working Trials competitor. The various scenting exercises were becoming more useful in daily life and on one occasion, on the seventeenth fairway on the Medal course, he mystified my companions and two other golfers by his scenting skills. My left-handed slice from the tee headed for the semi-rough between the seventeenth and second fairways. It was late in the evening and the

two other golfers were practising on the second fairway. My ball landed near some half-a-dozen practice balls and, as I arrived at the scene, one of the golfers asked me what ball I was playing. I replied, 'A Bromford.' The other golfer said, 'That's it over there, a Bromford black spot.' I explained that my ball was a blue spot. The golfer had a look, but could find no blue spot and said I must be wrong. I looked at Quest and said, 'Come on son, let's go and find it.' He sniffed at each ball in turn but did not recognize any as mine. However, some five yards (4.5m) away was an unkept bunker with heavy grass round it – the sort of place that would typically attract my golf ball. I directed Quest into the area and asked him to search it. He knew his job, and was in his element. Nose to the ground, he covered the area, stopped and stood over his find – he was not allowed to pick up golf balls. Sure enough, it was my blue spot Bromford. The two golfers were completely mystified and one asked how Quest had been able to tell one ball from another. 'Only he can answer that,' was my reply.

Training for Scenting Work

German Shepherd Dogs have inherited very strong capabilities in the world of scenting, and the potential for training the breed in the various activities for professional applications is well known. In the competitive field of work, German Shepherd owners were the first to appreciate the value of their breed's scenting ability. In the 1920s the Alsatian Sheep, Police and Army Dog Society started to run Working Trials. It is now many years

A tracking Shepherd of the future.

since the name 'Alsatian' was dropped from the title and replaced with 'Associated'. The Shepherd people opened the door and helped to train owners with many other breeds.

Over many years the police and civilians have worked hand in hand in training ventures and in the field of competition. I gained both my Kennel Club certificates to make Quest a W.T. P.D. Champion under two police sergeants, Sgt Terry Kane of Leeds and Sgt Wilf McGorrigan of Durham. I have also officiated at many trials where I have awarded qualifications and K.C. certificates to police dog handlers. This close co-operation went further in the early days before many police forces had built up their own dog sections. Quest's sire, Rab, and some of the Shepherds before him, owned by Jack Grant, were unofficially used by Dundee City Police to track intruders after a break-in, or to find a missing person. One particular inspector had great faith in the

capabilities of Jack's Shepherds and he proved to be very helpful to the force. I believe that in those early days other civilians were equally successful in different parts of the country.

Tracking is possibly the most fascinating feature of scenting work. From my earliest days with German Shepherds I wanted to know more and more about the subject. There was little in writing, only Colonel Konrad Most's book, *Training Dogs: A Manual* (*see* Further Reading), which did help to give me a start. I listened to anybody who seemed to know anything, but now realize how little I got from most of these sources. With the exception of two or three knowledgeable people, it was the blind leading the blind.

I was very lucky. Quest was a natural. He was the one who taught me. He did not need me to bring out his tracking instincts and my greatest achievement was the fact that I did nothing to ruin the potential of this amazing dog. It is pecu-

Tegan being prepared for a training track.

liar that it was training for the 'Sit and stay' that brought his interest in tracking to my attention. One particular area I used for obedience training was a local field of grass which was not being used by the farmer. Quest was probably about seven or eight months old and was well advanced for his age in the 'Sit/stay' exercise. I left him at the 'Sit' while I walked right round the perimeter of the field, a distance of some 300 to 400 yards (270–360m). Quest never budged during the training for this exercise, but on his release after my return he would put his nose down and follow my scent path right round the field and back to me.

There are other German Shepherds like him, others with the same enthusiasm and the same strong natural desires. However, these dogs create their own problems. Professional working dogs and civilian Working Trials dogs have to stop when they are tracking to indicate any articles dropped by the criminal or competition track-layer. Dogs like Quest have no inclination to indicate or stop for anything that is going to interfere with their concentration. They just want to track and track. I had a super tracking dog and

during those early days I did not appreciate the importance of stopping for these dropped articles. Eventually the realization of my errors took time to correct.

Track training was such fun. Any piece of ground would do. I knew little about the effect of ground that was contaminated with other scents. I did not know about the problems of other people or cattle on the ground before or after I had laid a track. One evening I laid a track on a piece of rough ground in the area known locally as Lovers' Loan (that should have told me something!). I returned about half-an-hour later with Quest, put on his harness and allowed him to start. He followed the scent path beautifully and was oblivious to anything around him – including the courting couple he stepped over half-way round the track. The couple were speechless and I could only mutter an apology as I walked round them.

One October Saturday evening when Quest was two years old and had qualified U.D.Ex., we had been visiting my mother and father. It was dark, and time to get the girls home for bed. My van was parked in the lane at the top of the garden. There were no lights as I went up the path to bring the van round to the front of the house. As I was opening the van door I noticed a man in a cap and trench coat standing under a tree where Dad's kennels had been situated before he retired. He had no business to be there. There was no reason for anybody to be on this piece of derelict ground on a dark evening. The situation looked rather suspicious, but I felt it would be wise to have Quest's company before challenging this guy. I went back to the house for Quest and told my father what was going on. It was an ideal evening for a burglary; many people were out. Dad agreed that there was no sense in keeping a German Shepherd and barking myself. Returning to the van, we found the man had gone, but where? I had no idea from which direction he had come, or where he had gone. The tracking harness was in the van and this seemed an ideal opportunity for a practical tracking exercise.

When you lay your own tracks for your dog in training or you have the track-layer at hand, mistakes can be corrected as and when they occur. In trials, the track has a known starting place, and knowing the direction of the walk in to the start gives you the opportunity to help your dog if need be. This situation was completely different. This was a novice dog and handler. It would be easy to backtrack from the tree in the wrong direction instead of following the scent path created by the mystery man after he had left the tree, and we would not know we were wrong. Now was the time to put theory into practice.

The sight of the harness always got Quest excited. He reckoned he was born to track. I took him to within a couple of yards of the tree and fitted the harness round his body. As the line was clipped to the harness he went forward, head down, to pick up the scent. He turned to the left and pulled hard into the harness. The scent was strong, no more than ten minutes old. An interested dog with proper training should not go wrong in these conditions. He followed the scent path across rough ground that had, at one time, been my father's livelihood, then on to the edge of a raspberry field. After a little cast to check his left side he turned and picked up the track to the right. He continued strongly at a very fast walking pace. After some 200 yards (180m), he stopped and looked up to his left. The mystery man was standing between the drills of raspberries, no more than three paces from us. I said, 'What the hell are you doing here?' Surprised to find a tracking German Shepherd in front of him and no doubt thinking 'police', he replied in very uncertain voice that he was waiting for his pal.

'Where's your pal?' This came out with the voice of authority. It is amazing how confident you can feel when you have a Shepherd by your side.

'He's along there somewhere.'

Now, this was a break in concentration for Quest. He had tracked to his objective. We would normally finish at that. Would he restart? A trained working police dog would take such a break in his stride, but we were in new territory. Quest responded with a little cast, then picked up another track. I was so busy concentrating on Quest I thought little about why the men were here or why one of them had gone on alone. I was too excited about our tracking success, and had little thought of where the track would take me, or what I would do at the end. This should be police business, not mine. We continued along the edge of the field and turned right between

A Police Dog having completed a track at civilian Working Trials.

some allotments to a large shed at the top of a garden. The other man was there, in the intimate company of a young lady. Knowing every family in the street and not recognizing either of them, I knew that they had no right to be there. Again, I said, 'What are you doing here?' Taken completely by surprise, they immediately parted with a rather sheepish 'Sorry'. With clothes rearranged, they departed smartly down the garden path and out of the front gate of number 69. Quest and I were more than pleased with our evening's work, and I doubt if that couple would make use of the area again.

Trackers – Natural and Otherwise

When I consider the tracking involvement of my other German Shepherds and those of family and friends, they probably cover the full spectrum of natural interest in the subject. Although all Shepherds can track, some are more natural than others; some are natural but don't realize it. These are the dogs who need to have that little door in their brain opened. Their tracking instinct is dormant. They can follow the scent path of another dog, or that of any other creature, but they have no inclination to concentrate for any length of time on a human scent. This dormant instinct must be brought to life if they are going to enjoy the real pleasures of their heritage.

As we have seen in Chapter 6, German Shepherds are generally short-sighted and I believe this encourages them to use their noses and concentrate on scent instead. However there are Shepherds who are long-sighted, and this seems to diminish their reliance on their scenting ability. I have already mentioned Tanya's long-sightedness, and there were great

The dedicated tracker.

difficulties in getting her to concentrate for any length of time on a track. After she gained her U.D.Ex., I gave up. Training bitches to track where and when I want has never been my strong point. I think I have always been too easy on the female members of my family.

I have learned a great deal from my bitches, but it may be that I have more desire to succeed with a male dog. Callum was an example. His desire to track was at rock bottom. He was a natural at everything else: obedience control brought out no problems, his agility was excellent until his hip gave way and protection work was so natural. But the powers of concentration for tracking must have been in short supply when he came into the world. A dog must want to track; he must have the will to concentrate. I have seen one Shepherd who had been taught to track without enjoyment. I judged the result, but did not like what I saw. He was not a happy dog. I do not know how the handler achieved this level of concentration and it is probably better not to know.

With Callum it was a slow process in building up concentration until we reached

his limit. He could work a fresh track for some 350 yards (315m), with the last fifty (45m) being done at a push. It was with Callum that I fully appreciated that the last fifty yards on a track was as important as the first fifty. Nobody in trials talked of such a thing in those days, and having been spoilt by Quest's abilities I was involved in a new learning curve. The track lengths were kept down to under 300 yards (270m) and I studied Callum's staying power. Eventually, distances were very gradually increased and so long as he was powering on at the end we were winning. My greatest pleasure was his three-hour-old track in Championship T.D. We won the cup for the best track and search, and the judge said he went like an express train. That was music to my ears.

Environment can therefore play a major role in a Shepherd's tracking abilities. Early entry into Obedience competitions is one factor which can have a disastrous effect on a dog's tracking capabilities. Dogs who have been pushed into strict heel work at an early age tend to look to their handlers for guidance and support. They lose the measure of independence

Tegan finding the article on the track.

that enables them to think for themselves. Quest and a few others may have been exceptions to the rule. He did have quite a bit of heel training in his earlier days but its effects were tempered when tracking took up so much of our interest while he was still a junior.

Searching

Quartering the undergrowth for missing articles is another element of police work which also comes into civilian working trials. This can be mastered by any pet German Shepherd. In trials the exercise involves a 25-yard (23m) square marked by a post at each corner to identify the area. Four articles are placed in the undergrowth in this area and the dog is given five minutes to find them. The articles are usually relatively small – I have seen all four being put into a matchbox. The articles are scented by the search steward without the dog's knowledge, and the dog is expeceted to identify the items in the area that have a fresh human scent. The training for this exercise does have its uses.

On one occasion, I had lost my new Parker 51 pen. I did not know if it had been in my jacket pocket when we took the children out for a walk with Quest and our new pup, Tanya. When we got home I realized my pen was not in my pocket. We searched the house, but there was no sign of it. I could only think that it had fallen out of my pocket during that walk. We thought of the route we had taken and what we had been doing. While walking through an estate, there was a large area some fifty yards (45m) square covered with heavy grass. We had stopped there and had some fun with the girls and the dogs. That seemed the most likely spot to have lost the pen.

About two hours after the walk I cycled back to the estate, with Quest trotting beside me. I set him to work but it was a lot to expect of him, with such a large area to cover. It seemed the perfect place for a pen that did not want to be found. Quest worked away for about fifteen minutes, much longer than he had ever been asked during any training session. I was thinking of giving up. After all, I did not know for certain that the pen was in that area. I was beginning to wonder if I had

Hidden persons

Indicating the presence of a 'criminal' hidden up a tree.

Quartering and searching for a hidden person is another task in police work and civilian trials. Although body scent is a principal feature in locating the hidden person, this is an air scenting operation. Air scenting, in itself, should be a simple operation for any self-respecting dog. The hard work is in teaching the dog to quarter wide areas of ground under the direction of the handler. The dog must then give vocal recognition of his find and remain with him. He may also have to defend himself. Although this is certainly a scenting operation, the use of his nose is the easiest part for the dog and German Shepherds take it in their stride.

brought it home from work. At last Quest's head gave a smart jerk round, his head went down into the grass and I thought, 'Bingo, He's found it!' He turned and immediately came back to me with his find. However, as he came back I couldn't see anything sticking out of his mouth. A pen would be visible. I put my hand down and he dropped his treasured find into my hand. It was an earring. Quest had done an excellent job, but I was disappointed. The pen could be anywhere. It had been a birthday present and now it was lost. We set off for home to break the news to Irene.

When I got home I let her see Quest's find. She immediately put her hand to her ear and said, 'Where did you find it?' She had not missed it, and I did not let on that I had not recognized the earring to be hers.

Another similar incident occurred at one of my evening outdoor training sessions. I had the use of a field, and Miss Moncrieffe turned up in her new Jaguar car. She had her German Shepherd, just out of quarantine, with her. After the training session we all returned to our cars, and Miss Moncrieffe said, 'I've lost my car keys.'

She checked in every pocket and we searched the car park: no keys. Somebody said that they must be in the field somewhere. Caro was the only searching dog there and Miss Moncrieffe asked if I thought he could find them. It was a daunting thought. It was a large field, and I did not want to raise her hopes of finding the keys when the odds seemed to be against us. However, there was really no option and we went back into the field. We started searching and worked our way down the field. Luck was with us: about forty yards (35m) from the entrance to the field Caro's head arrowed in to the long tufted grass at the edge, and out it came with the keys.

Many trials people have had the opportunity of applying this skill to help find lost items of personal value. I heard of one search steward at a trials who lost her watch, but she had no idea when or in which field. The following day they were competing in the same fields, with the search squares located in the same general areas as before. The competing German Shepherd, while searching for the four articles, brought out the lost watch unharmed and working.

Scent Discrimination

Our principal interest in scent discrimination is for Obedience competitions. The police in some European countries do make use of the procedure to try and iden-tify a criminal by the scent left behind at the scene of a crime. I think the opportunity to make practical use of this procedure would be quite limited and we should restrict the application of scent discrimination to the top class of Obedience.

In competitions, the grading of discriminating starts with the dog being asked to detect an article (now a piece of cloth) containing the handler's own scent. This cloth is placed on the ground with others, some of which are neutral and others decoy-scented. This should be quite a simple task for any self-respecting German Shepherd. However, it is more exacting for the dog to find an article carrying the scent of a selected stranger. Although this is a simple task for the dog, it is difficult for the owner to convey his requirements to his dog.

Quest was the only dog with whom I trained and competed in the top Obedience class and he was reliable in this exercise. I can recall only one occasion when he failed to identify and return with the correctly scented cloth in the Obedience ring. But he was much more at home out in the fields tracking or searching.

We had fun at the lower end of the competition requirements with our various dogs, and were also involved in many club demonstrations held for the general public. It was always an eye-catcher to see the dogs investigating each piece of cloth to identify the correct one. The public did not realize how simple this exercise was for a trained German Shepherd.

CHAPTER 10

Environmental Influences

There is no doubt that the breeding of your German Shepherd – his genetic background – is an essential factor in what makes your dog what he is. But whether or not the breeder has given proper consideration to the various characteristics of the breed, it is the environmental factors that complete the job. In other words, the dog's breeding constitutes the foundation upon which it is the owner's responsibility to build.

Many a puppy of ideal breeding has been ruined by environmental factors at some stage in its life. On the other hand, a number of puppies from inappropriate breeding have been nursed through the problem stage of their lives to become good ambassadors of the breed.

Unfortunately, breeders are expected to take responsibility for all of the breed's problems. At the same time, some breeders are too prepared to blame new owners for problems that are obviously a result of their own actions – a mating that should never have taken place, or an initial environment that was unsuited to the upbringing of young stock. Nevertheless, it is a buyer's market; and as such some research into the breeding of litters and the reputation of the breeders should minimize the possibility of your being sold a 'pup'.

If we are prepared to take off our rose-coloured spectacles we shall realize that none of our own dogs, past or present, is perfect. That does not detract from our affection for them. It is purely a case of recognizing the facts of life, and being honest and realistic in our assessment of our dogs. Indeed, this is an essential part of preparing for training: if we can be honest about our dogs' strengths and weaknesses, good and bad points, we will be better able to make the most of the dog's potential.

Choosing a Dog

We buy or breed our pup, or perhaps accept an older one from the breeding kennel, or take a rescue dog. It is our choice and we live by it. We then create the environment to achieve the best with the material we have. The objective is to have a sound companion who may need to be a good working partner as well. Your choice of dog will be influenced by your reasons for having a German Shepherd.

Firstly you recognize why you want a Shepherd. Is it to be a dog or a bitch? Is he to be a companion in the home? Is he also to be trained for one of the various

The final choice: which shall it be?

forms of competition such as breed showing, Working Trials, Obedience or Agility? Perhaps the dog will also be given a job of work to do, as a professional. But if he is not to be a companion in addition to one of these 'also's', please think again. The German Shepherd is a thinking animal who needs your companionship and attention if he is to be content.

For most owners, the beginning of a dog's life is not the planning of a mating or a birth, but the moment that they introduce a Shepherd into their home. Should it be a young puppy or one of the many alternatives? Most people either want a puppy, or they want one that has passed the so-called puppy problem stage (although all too often they find they have taken on real problems – *see* Chapter 2).

I have often been asked for advice on buying a German Shepherd, and generally find it difficult to give the kind of answers that are wanted. Would-be owners usually want confirmation of decisions they have already made. I find it easier to give details of my philosophy on bringing a Shepherd into our own household, although of course not everyone's circumstance are exactly like mine.

My first aim is to take on a puppy of about eight weeks old. In theory, I want one that will grow up to embody the characteristics defined by the Breed Standard and therefore good enough to show. However, latterly we have finished up with one (that we bred ourselves) that was well over the Standard in height, and one that has a long coat. We have parted with neither.

A puppy left to his own devices (above) can be destructive. Better that he destroys an old container (below) than a personal item.

I also aim to choose dogs with strength of character and good working ability. Again, we have not always made the wisest choice, but they have all been excellent companions. We would not have exchanged them for others.

Over the years we have enjoyed having a dog and a bitch at home, about four or five years apart in age. A youngster would come into our home when an existing dog was getting on in years or had departed. It is the greatest tribute to the last Shepherd to replace the departed with the vibrancy of youth.

We prefer to do without the probable clash of personalities that can occur between two animals of the same sex sharing the prime time of their lives. Two adult males can be a problem and two females can be a bigger problem. All too often, I have seen an owner having to part with a Shepherd because of dominance problems that have become apparent between two of the same sex when they reach maturity. Litter-sisters kept together can be a real problem, especially if both have similar levels of dominance. For example, my own bitch Ceilidh, and my daughter's, Tegan, are not related and do not live together. There is a two-year difference in age, and they are both dominant. They can play in the open without a cross word, but to have both in the same room without supervision would be a recipe for a physical confrontation. Both have the same attitude, best described by, 'She is my best friend, but I hate her.'

Dogs and Families

Although our puppies become family pets, I train them for competition work, so it is important that the family do not become

a distraction. Quest was truly a family dog. He would herd us all together if we were separated while out for a walk. When competing in Obedience, Irene and the girls were a distraction and, while working in championship class 'C', I would go to the show without them. For some obscure reason they were never a distraction at Working Trials. Even in the top stake, and competing for the Challenge Certificate, Quest was never distracted by the presence of the family. The more placid atmosphere of trials, and my own relaxed attitude, may have given Quest more confidence.

At this early stage in my competitive career I was often given advice by my competitors. One urged me never to bring the family to training sessions, while another recommended keeping the dog in a kennel during the day and taking him out only for exercise and training. I felt that if that was what it took to win, I would rather give up competing. Although I ignored the advice, Quest became a champion, which proves that ultimately you must follow your own instincts.

The question of preferred loyalties in the family arose when Tanya joined us as a ten-week-old 'butterball'. As already described in Chapter 2, she was in our home for a full week before I could give her any attention myself, and she became very much Irene's dog. Tanya loved her family, but Irene was always on her mind when I was training her. Tracking was always a problem in training. Tanya was crafty, and at one competition when Irene was present, she worked the first leg of the track beautifully, turned left (wrong direction), then turned left again towards Irene who was standing near the start. Her head never came up. There was no scent path, but it was the way back to her mum.

Duncan was a typical mischievous puppy.

I finally qualified Tanya by leaving Irene at home. The lesson was obvious: after that, we were careful to introduce puppies into the household only at times when I would be at home for at least the first five days. I was there to feed the puppies and see to all their needs, to put them in their place if need be, and to play with them. It all paid dividends. I had their full attention for training and competitions, but they were still 'family dogs.'

Circumstances made Duncan an exception. He was one puppy we bred and kept. I was at work all day, and for five days a week Irene helped Isla to mother her pups from the day they were born. She weaned them on to solid foods – she did everything – and was there for Duncan when the other pups left the nest. When Duncan was four months old I was rushed to hospital for an emergency operation and was out of commission for a few weeks. During this spell at home I real-

ized I was losing Duncan. He was becoming Irene's dog. Fortunately I retired shortly after, and regained my place as Duncan's number one companion.

In the pet home, these situations are of little importance – and often go unnoticed – but if the German Shepherd is to be worked, his number one companion must be the handler who works him.

Children

Great care must always be taken to ensure that both children and Shepherds act responsibly when in each other's company. Children can be their own worst enemies when there are dogs around. They should be encouraged to be calm and quiet, not to throw their arms around or make jerky and quick movements. Any dog that is not accustomed to such antics can act unpredictably and could be a danger to the children. At the end of the day,

Quest loved playing with the children.

the dog will usually be held responsible for any mishap, even if the child has tormented the dog. German Shepherd owners must accept that owning a Shepherd carries added responsibilities because of the breed's perceived reputation.

Two five-year-old boys, who lived close by, came to see Callum one day. Although he was a hard dog, he was great with children. One little boy took him by the collar and said, 'I will just take him for Mummy to meet him.' Callum would have gone with him, but I decided that it wasn't a good idea – I could imagine his mother's reaction on seeing this little fellow going into the house with a huge German Shepherd in tow.

The faith of children with Shepherds they know is a pleasure to watch. Sharon was the eight-year-old daughter of a friend. Although shy and rather reserved, she was prepared to play a small but important part in a BBC television series, 'The Mad Death', about the accidental introduction of rabies into Scotland. Caro played the part of a dog that was suspected of being rabid and that had escaped, with others, from a compound. He was being hunted down in the scene that involved Sharon.

I had been approached to supply a German Shepherd, and also to find an eight-year-old child, for the build-up to a scene where the dog attacked a child. The end result was breathtaking, with Caro darting into attack Sharon and leave her with a badly bitten cheek. It took a little time to devise a method of simulating the attack in a way that would make it look very realistic without any danger to the child. We tried a number of approaches to give Sharon the confidence to meet Caro head on. We eventually decided that a simple retrieve would be the exercise on which to base our approach.

I made up a dummy retrieve article with a piece of plastic tubing about an inch (2.5cm) in diameter and some six inches (15cm) in length. I then wrapped it in a few layers of sacking, and threaded a piece of cord the middle. This became Caro's play toy. It was used as a bite-bar for a tug-of-war, with me on the other end. Caro was always allowed to win the battle. Every time the 'bite-bar' was brought out, he wanted it. Sometimes it was used for a tug-of-war, and at others for a simple fun retrieve.

During filming only one take was required. Sharon was kneeling in a clear-

Caro, and Sharon with the dummy retrieve article, preparing for their part in the television series, 'The Mad Death'.

ing in a wood when the 'attack' took place. She was holding the ends of the cord, with her hands well away from the 'bite-bar', but it was close to her chest, out of view of the camera. Caro was sent in to retrieve his bar. There were no knots or loops on the cord so the bar just slipped through her hands as Caro retrieved it. In the cutting room, the scene was ended before the bar came into view.

The Older Dog

Growing old happens to each one of us, and all too often we fail to appreciate that with increasing age comes wisdom as well as infirmity. It may be a very gradual process for us – and a dog's own ageing process may appear to him to be equally gradual – but in our own life-time dogs seem to age very quickly.

Isla and Duncan during the summer of 1991. We lost both of them within a space of eight weeks.

When training dogs for competition work, breed showing or a professional career, there seems to be only a short space of time between mental maturity and the first signs of physical ailments. Generally, by the age of seven, they are over the hill as regards the various fields of activity. If they have been real companions, they and we can still enjoy their well-earned retirement, so long as they are not cast aside and forgotten when the next generation takes their place.

Retirement

A police dog usually retires to become a family pet in the household that has been his home. More often than not he will be more cosseted than during his working life. The competition dog usually enjoys the same privileges, but how do you know when the time for retirement has come? To most Shepherds in retirement, continuing with some training is much the same as the human pensioner filling in his time with past or new hobbies. It is a delight to watch an oldie being asked to do a round of work after he has watched his replacement going through the basics. It is as though the oldies say, 'Why waste your time on him? Just let him see my polished performance.' They are only too happy to be given an opportunity to show off.

Unfortunately, some owners do not know when to stop competing. There are always cups to be won and rosettes to collect. They like to think it is for the benefit of the dog, but it is usually the personal ego trip that maintains the desire to win. Having said this, I do know that deciding when to retire a dog can be difficult. Quest was seven years of age when I felt the time had come. He had started his showing career in the breed ring at the age of six months, and competed in Obedience at ten months and in Working Trials at seventeen months.

After a very successful career, Quest was, at the age of seven, a member of the South team in the great North v. South annual match for German Shepherds. He had already competed for the South the previous year, when he had won the gold medal for the best all-round performance; and he had been in the North team two years earlier when we had lived in Scotland. This event was a combination of exercises from both Obedience and

Working Trials. The dogs had to be really good to cover the variety in the exercises.

Quest's agility was always on top form, but he was starting to struggle on the six-foot scale-jump during this final match. At that moment I decided that he had done enough, and would not be asked to jump to the full requirements again. Although we competed in fun events in his declining years, the agility tests were a thing of the past. Eventually Quest lost his hearing, but when I could catch his attention, the hand signals he had learned from his days in training played an important part in our revised approach to communicating.

Letting Go

Making the decision to let a dog finally go is almost always a difficult one. One has to be honest with oneself about the reason for allowing the life of a close friend to be extinguished.

Everybody has their own ideas about calling in the vet for that final and fateful injection. For myself, the decision is governed by the dog's quality of life and his prospects for the future. Without the prospect of recovery, and reasonable quality of life, I cannot see a dog suffer. Having said this, there are some cases that are not so cut and dried, and then it can be difficult to judge what the dog actually feels. I do not know what goes through a dog's mind, but I find that I can tell much by the look in my own dog's eyes. When I see that look, I will say to the vet that I think it is time to let him go. With the decision made, I will stay with him until I feel that the spirit has left the body.

I seem to be able to time it right because the vet has always been in full agreement, except for one occasion. We lost Isla with liver cancer when she was eight years old.

Some eight weeks later her three-year-old son, Duncan, picked up a kidney infection. From the first signs until he died was just one week. His last four days were spent in the surgery. We were with him every day, and on the Friday afternoon we could take no more. The end seemed inevitable. I said to the vet, 'Is it not time to let him go?' She asked us to give him another twenty-four hours. She had put his mother to sleep just weeks before. Two hours later she phoned to say that Duncan had died. I was not with him at the end.

When a dog is so ill, the company of his best friend at the end may not be appreciated – we do not know what dogs think – but my absence at such a crucial time certainly affected me. I do not blame the vet, but my assessment had been right, and I should have been with Duncan when he died.

To make matters worse, we were now without a German Shepherd Dog for the first time in thirty-three years. The house lost its sparkle until Ceilidh arrived on the scene.

Developing Innate Talent

Moulding a dog's innate talents and potential should be the prime function of any owner. It is not necessary to train and work the dog – although they would all benefit from the more active mental approach to life – but owners should at least ensure that dogs do not use their capabilities to the detriment of the owner or the breed.

Each talent plays a part in the dog's life. His temperament and loyalty may cause him to be overprotective and, if this is not properly controlled or channelled, he can easily become the dominant member of the family. Such a dog can then become responsible *for*, rather than *to*, his owner's family. An over-keen noseworker can become obsessed by scenting trails and therefore oblivious to the owner's actions or any attempt at verbal control.

Ceilidh was trained for Working Trials for two years or more. Physical infirmity prevented me from continuing with serious training but she was used at college for training students for a further four years. Every time she was taken by a new student she enjoyed the attention and the work-out. As one student put it, Ceilidh's mind had been activated by the earlier programmes of training. The student was quite correct. Stimulating the mind of a youngster brings out the intelligence that could otherwise lie dormant or could be used against the community if left to it's own devices.

Sometimes, certain capabilities or talents will remain unrecognized in a German Shepherd. They lie dormant until something clicks in the dog's mind, opening the door to a more interesting life. Puppies that are not introduced to fun and games in early life can turn out to be very dull dogs. Jeza was one, there was no fun in her life before I took her on at the age of about six months. Toys were meaningless to her. She had no idea how to play with me on the floor. Training opened the door to a change in her life. Teaching the retrieve was a long, slow process because she had no aptitude for a bit of fun. It took a whole year to induce a retrieve to competition standard.

Tracking with Jeza was a nightmare for me, until I discovered by accident that a disc in flight was like a bird to her; she was a real country lass. Six-inch (15cm) discs on the ends of reels of elastic were her favourite. She loved to go for them when they went slicing through the air; and to

see a disc in my hand was enough to get her excited. A door in that dormant section of her mind had been opened. She would now do anything for her disc. No other toy had the same effect. I could now get her to track for them and search for them. She would never be a top-class noseworker, but she enjoyed what was asked of her.

Ceilidh was the opposite. When she came home at eight weeks and I got down on the floor to play, she knew all about it and she was rough. When I phoned the breeder to tell her Ceilidh was settling in I asked whether the children had been playing with her. She said they had, but wondered how I knew. She went on to explain that she had brought the pups into the house for short periods when the children were home from school. They were sensible children and they had given the pups a great start to their lives.

Strengths and Weaknesses

Each Shepherd is born with his own strengths and weaknesses. Ideally, the owner's response to both will be to capitalize on the existing strengths and do whatever they can to build strengths out of the weaknesses.

A weakness in scenting ability or in the inclination to retrieve may be of no concern to the pet dog owner. And a shortage of courage may well be considered an asset to the owner who is more at ease with a timid animal. However, anybody with a sense of real respect for the breed would wish to create an environment that would counter any weaknesses that cast a doubt on his Shepherd's character.

A weakness that is evident at an early stage in a pup's life may be owed purely to immaturity and lack of experience. I was rather disappointed with Caro once, when he was about nine or ten months old and we were confronted with a group of disruptive teenagers. I tried to stand my ground, and expected Caro to show some signs of resentment towards their attitude. One cheeky youngster came over, patted him, told him he was a good boy and asked his name. Caro was quite indifferent to the situation. He gave no signs of backing or support. A few months later, without encouragement from me, Caro became much more perceptive of situations and took a great interest in events while we were watching a training session on protection work. His protection instincts had been awakened, and they would now have to be controlled.

Although Quest was a more gentle dog than Caro, his protection instincts showed themselves when he was about a year old. Alec, a good friend, was visiting. He picked up our young daughter, Joyce, and started dancing to the music. Quest was up in a flash and made it clear to Alec that that was enough. He put her down and Quest relaxed – problem solved.

Quest was eventually introduced to protection work when he was three years old. Although his attitude towards Alec had shown a protective instinct, the work was never his strongest point for when he went in for the bite it was with an apology. In time, experience and a strengthening of his resolve in this work turned him into a harder biter, although he could not match the hard character of Callum when it came to strength of bite. On the other hand, when it came to tracking, Callum could never show the resolve and dedication of Quest.

One of Callum's strengths was his reaction to gunfire. In common with many others in the trials scene I had a .22mm starting pistol to acclimatize the dogs to the sound of gunfire. One day, when Callum had been with us for about a week, he was in the garden with Quest and Tanya minding his own business. This nine-week-old pup was an arrogant little soul; nothing upset him. I went to the other end of the garden and put off a shot. No reaction. I repeated this about six paces away. Still no reaction. I stood over Callum, pointed the pistol upwards and pressed the trigger. Again, no reaction. I called his name and he looked up at me; he was not deaf.

There was no doubt that unusual noises were not going to bother this young fellow. He was about eight months old when I brought the gun out again. We were walking the dogs on the beach with the tide at its lowest, and a great expanse of sand for the dogs to enjoy. There was the usual cold wind coming in from the North Sea, and fortunately we were wearing heavy parkas. As Callum ran past I fired the pistol and, before I realized what was happening, he turned, hit me on the chest and took a mouthful of parka.

From that day, the gun was there to be attacked. This strong and dedicated reaction was part of his breeding – not environmental conditioning. It was a strength to be controlled, but also one to capitalize on in future training.

Capitalizing on existing strengths is just as important as building strengths out of weaknesses. If a particular Shepherd in training is a natural at any aspect of work, I believe we have a duty to make him a master of his craft. Strengths give both dog and owner the confidence to work on the aspects of work for which the dog is less well motivated. Confidence breeds confidence, and both the dogs and ourselves are beneficiaries.

The car is a second home to our dogs.

Ability to Fit in

Moving house, especially into a completely new environment, is stressful for all of us. To some extent it may be exciting but there is always uncertainty in change, especially when there is also a new job to cope with. Our dogs are no different, being creatures of habit. I wonder how much thought is given to our pets when we move from one area to another? If they are accustomed to holidays away from home, a permanent move will be easier for them to accept.

Although the familiarity of all house furnishings play their part in helping a dog to feel comfortable, carpets and rugs matter most to a home-loving German Shepherd. In days gone by, the carpets were moved with the rest of the furnishings and once the carpet was down, the dog would be happy. He would recognize the scents and smells as home. Today, most carpets are fitted and are sold with the house. Moving into a new home with carpets bearing the scents of the previous occupants, especially

if they had a dog, can prolong your own dog's settling-in period. It is only when his own scents and those of his family prevail that he will settle in properly.

When we have moved house, we have found that putting down our own rugs has helped our dogs to feel at home more quickly.

Neighbours

Most new neighbours show apprehension at the arrival of German Shepherds next door. They know of their reputation but have probably never experienced the breed at first hand. We have moved home several times during the past forty years. and with each move it has seemed to us that the neighbours accepted our Shepherds without concern. In time, though, many confessed that they initially had reservations when we arrived with our 'Alsatians'.

It was the dogs themselves who became ambassadors for the breed. They quickly broke down any resistance to their presence. One old lady had great reservations

Quest often travelled on the old Tay ferry.

about our three Shepherds moving in next door. However, she now acknowledges that, with an open field bordering the garden to the rear, she felt much more secure with our dogs 'on watch' at night. A bark in the middle of the night would tell us that somebody was passing along the fence bordering the field. There were no burglaries at our end of the street.

Travelling and Traffic

German Shepherds generally like to travel. In the car they can enjoy being in our company; if they are in training, or going to trials or shows, they know the routine and anticipate events with relish.

Unfortunately, their start to life in a car is not always to their liking. Travel-sickness is something that many puppies have to overcome. If my own pups can be used as a guide, most were troubled with travel-sickness during their initial jour-

ney home. With some of them, this continued on subsequent trips.

It can take considerable perseverance to cure a dog of travel sickness. In many cases, the condition is caused by stress rather than a physiological reaction to motion, and in such cases you can help the dog to overcome the problem by teaching him to feel more positive about being in the car. Sit in the car with him, but without going anywhere, and give him a titbit. Take him on frequent but very short car journeys to somewhere that he will enjoy being – such as the park – and praise him on arrival. On your return home, give him a titbit and praise him again. In most cases, dogs that associate car journeys with pleasant experiences are less likely to be sick than those who travel only to the vet or on long excursions to unfamiliar places.

Initially, when Quest was a youngster, we had to rely on public transport. He was never sick on the bus when leaving home but was sometimes sick on the homeward journey. Fortunately, we lived at the terminus and were able to clean it up before the bus made its return to town. He soon grew out of this phase and became an excellent traveller.

Quest did have one phobia about traffic. He would not blink an eye at the tube train coming into an Underground station, and he could stand by a level crossing when an express train came thundering down the line, but a heavy goods lorry passing on his side of the road would cause him to move away. He obviously had a 'thing' about the exhaust or the servo brakes, although none of us can recall any previous experience that could have caused this phobia.

Ceilidh spent her first eight weeks in a kennel at the bottom of a garden, adjacent to a cutting that contained a busy railway line. Not surprisingly after that, trains, however close, caused her no problem. Road traffic also caused little concern, but then, like all our dogs, she had been introduced to traffic at an early age.

Habits and Moods

German Shepherds are not creatures prone to mood swings. Overall, they are highly predictable.

Any signs of unpredictability are usually an indication of a change in circumstances, an injury or an illness. The Shepherd that does not come when called on the odd occasion is usually acting out of character because the circumstances at that moment have changed. Shepherds are creatures of habit, and these habits develop through their experiences of life.

Ceilidh knows that if she brings her large 'Kong' (heavy, rubber toy) to me in the evening I will put a few liver treats into it. She will take the Kong, put it on the floor, and turn it over so that the treats fall out. A little later, she will bring her small Kong and put it on my lap. The process with the liver treats is repeated. (I have always been an easy touch with the female members of the family.)

For the purposes of a writing project that I was working on, I bought an activity ball to assess its value. It is now Ceilidh's. After bringing the two Kongs in the evening she manages to get a canine tooth into the two holes of this large ball; she will then pick it up and dump it in my lap. I get up and put some small cubes of mixer food into the ball. She pushes it around the floor with her nose until all the pieces of food have fallen out and been eaten one by one. She then lies down as if

to say, 'That's all I'll get from him tonight.' I started the routine with the large Kong, but it was she who developed the idea to its further stages. She is a real thinker.

I have found my male Shepherds to be very predictable. Their attitudes to life and their performances in the field of work changed only with the experiences of the past. They made training so much easier. Success today would ensure success tomorrow, and a failure could be attributed to an obvious change in circumstances. It is possible that I could read my male dogs better than the bitches, could understand them and act in a manner that prevented problems from arising.

If a dog had a genetic weakness, I would take measures to make the best of it. Caro had a weakness in the 'Speak on command' exercise in Working Trials. This was worth a very valuable five marks in the Tracker Dog Stake and I always tried to salvage some marks from the expected zero. If we gained any marks it was because of ingenuity, not the dog's ability.

The bitches were quite different and there were times when I had no idea what kind of performance to expect. Hormone problems cause a moodiness that is never seen in male dogs. I could take a bitch to trials in the knowledge that she could carry out every exercise, and finish up apologizing to the judge for wasting his time with a performance that shamed me. On other occasions the bitches would work their hearts out and make me so proud of them.

Jeza and Ceilidh proved to be real problems and, even after spaying, it took a great deal of time before they achieved a reasonable degree of consistency. When the bitches are good they can be excellent, but I cannot read them. I have adored them, and they are lovely to have around, but their understanding of me has always

Ceilidh's understanding of me was greater than mine of her.

seemed to be much greater than my understanding of them.

Variety of Environments

German Shepherds have the versatility to fit into many different environments and carry out a great variety of tasks.

Apart from being ideal pets they can stimulate our own capabilities by the opportunities they offer for training. Working Trials, Obedience competitions, Agility and breed showing are all within the scope of Kennel Club activities. One or more of these activities can become a way of life for the pet dog owner.

Although training for the show ring does little, if anything, to test the intelligence of

the breed, it does create an interest for owners and can help to cement a sound companionship. However, if exhibitors wheel their dogs out for show, then return them to their kennels until the next show, they are not doing justice to their animals. I sometimes think that people who treat their dogs in this way should take up a sport like golf instead. After a round of golf you can put your clubs in a cupboard and forget about them until the next game.

Professionally, there are excellent outlets for our breed, including the police, security services and the armed forces. Search and rescue can be practised by professionals as well as amateurs. Fewer German Shepherds are now trained as guide dogs for the blind in the UK than in days gone by. The gundog breeds seem to have taken

(Above) *A Seeing Eye German Shepherd in training.* (Right) *The author being guided by a Seeing Eye German Shepherd.*

precedence. In America, Shepherds are still a popular breed for this purpose.

I recall paying a visit to the Seeing Eye operational base and administration head-quarters at Morristown, New Jersey. This visit was arranged by Don Arner, editor and publisher of *Off-Lead* magazine and also a German Shepherd enthusiast. Lois Fryston, editor of the *German Shepherd Review* was also one of our company. Our host was Eddie Outhaut, the head trainer, who was also a Schutzhund training enthusiast with his own Shepherd. It was interesting to meet a trainer who could master two completely different objectives in training German Shepherds.

The highlight of the visit was a session of practical training in the streets of Morristown. This was a busy little town, and the session reminded me of the guide dogs being trained at my home base of Broughty Ferry. On this occasion I was blind-folded and given a partially trained Shepherd as my guide. The trainer was by my side to ensure that nothing went wrong. This young Shepherd guided me down pavements, avoiding the trees lining the road. We also crossed intersections where I was more than aware of the traffic.

It was one of the most marvellous feel-ings I have ever had – the feeling of a dog in harness making decisions for me. It reminded me of tracking in the dark. It was a feeling of complete dependence in practical life-and-death situations. It takes a lot of trust for a blind person to put his life in the hands of a dog. No other work that I have done with dogs has given me such a feeling of gratitude to our breed. It was a privilege to be in the care of such an intelligent animal for that short period of time.

Postscript

I have written mainly about my own dogs and personal experiences because they are the source of so much of my information about the breed. I have often been asked which of the dogs I have owned was the best – a difficult question. Without implying any criticism of earlier dogs, I would probably say that the one living at the time the question is posed is the best. However, I think I have always been more in tune with my male dogs, for, as I have said, I find bitches more difficult to understand. Each of the males had his strengths and weaknesses but, like the bitches, each and every one has a special place in my own file of memories.

Having said this, special mention must be made of Quest, principally because he introduced me to this wonderful breed, but also because of his versatility. Such versatility may have been because he was our only dog for a number of years and therefore had the undivided attention of an enthusiastic novice. Everything that happened within our family centred on Quest.

At one stage, Col. Baldwin, the father of the breed in the UK, was quoted as saying that Quest was the 'best all-round German Shepherd in the country' at that time (the early 1960s). His success in Working Trials, Obedience and the show ring was a difficult act to follow, and I take it as a great honour to have had Quest singled out by such an eminent enthusiast of the breed.

Versatility like Quest's is a thing of the past – not that the dogs are incapable of diversifying. I would take great pleasure in seeing the owners of more Shepherds competing in the various fields that highlight their trainability, intelligence and structural qualities.

There have been dogs and bitches in the past who would certainly challenge Quest for the honour bestowed on him by Col. Baldwin. The famous father and son act, Terrie and Dankie of Glenvoca, were both Obedience and breed champions. They also qualified in the lower stakes in Working Trials. The Hankley bitches, Amaryllis and Andromeda, were a mother and daughter act: both were Working Trials and Obedience champions, and I believe both were entered in breed shows. These and others were great Shepherds in their day. Their breeding gave them a start in life, but it was the contribution from their environment with their owners that made them 'something special'.

We give so much to our dogs, but they give so much more in return. Any training with a German Shepherd means a steep learning curve for the owner. The dogs benefit, of course, but we, as owners, learn so much more about our dogs and about the breed in general. Training adds a new dimension to companionship: it makes for a true partnership.

Further Reading

Books

The Breed Standards:
  American (The American Kennel Club, New York).
  British (The Kennel Club, London).
  German (Federation Cynologique Internationale, Brussels).
Clutton-Brock, J., *A Natural History of Domesticated Mammals*, British Museum (1987).
Cree, J., *Nosework for Dogs*, Pelham Books (1988)
Training the German Shepherd Dog, The Crowood Press (1996).
Your Dog, The Crowood Press (1996).
Galton, F., *The First Steps towards the Domestication of Animals* (1865), trans. Ethnol. Society, London, N.S. 122–38. Reprinted in *Inquiries into Human Faculty* (1907), J.M. Dent
Most, K., *Training Dogs*: A Manual, Popular Dogs (1954).
Schwabacher, J. and Gray, T., *The Alsatian: The German Shepherd* Dog, Popular Dogs (1922).
Von Stephanitz, H., *The German Shepherd*, Deutsche Schafferhunde S.V (1951).
Wootton, B., *The German Shepherd Dog*, David & Charles (1988).

Magazines

Off-Lead, Barkleigh Productions, Inc.
German Shepherd Dog Review (breed magazine).

Appendices

I Principal Dogs Referred to in the Text

Pet Name	Registered Name	Sire and Dam
Quest	W.T.Ch. Quest of Ardfern C.D.Ex. U.D.Ex. P.D.Ex.. T.D.Ex. (March 1958 to October 1971)	S. Cresta of Aronbel C.D.Ex. U.D.Ex. P.D.Ex. T.D.Ex. D. Letton Questionnaire
Tanya	Spagnum of Brittas C.D.Ex. U.D.Ex. (November 1960 to October 1969)	S. Int. Ch. Ilex of Brittas D. Quixhilde of Brittas
Kerry	Wascana Irina of Ardfern (June 1964 to unknown)	S. W.T.Ch. Quest of Ardfern C.D.Ex. U.D.Ex. P.D.Ex. T.D.Ex. D. Wascana Cheiron
Callum	Shadowsquad Callum of Ardfern C.D.Ex. U.D.Ex. W.D.Ex. P.D.Ex. (January 1967 to November 1976)	S. Billo vom Saynbach Sch.H.II. D. Honeysuckle of Brittas
Jeza	Dunmonaidh Hebe of Ardfern C.D.Ex. U.D.Ex. W.D.C. of Merit (November 1970 to October 1982)	S. Peregrine of Dunmonaidh D. Hexe of Dunmonaidh
Caro	Tanfield Atholl of Ardfern C.D.Ex. U.D.Ex. W.D.Ex. T.D.Ex. (December 1976 to October 1988)	S. Vikkas Tanfield Caro D. Linda vom Haus Musshafen Sch.H.I.
Isla	Vikkas Electra of Ardfern C.D.Ex. U.D.Ex. W.D.C. of Merit (January 1983 to June 1991)	S. Vikkas Alaric D. Nana vom Hambachtal

Pet Name	Registered Name	Sire and Dam
Strachan	Vikkas Tiberius C.D.Ex. U.D.Ex. W.D.Ex., T.D.Ex. (August 1986 —)	*S.* Aro von Weisenborn *D.* Tanfield Verda of Vikkas
Duncan	Ardfern Duncan C.D.Ex. U.D.Ex. W.D.C. of Merit (June 1988 to September 1991)	*S.* Vicksburg Yalk *D.* Vikkas Electra of Ardfern C.D.Ex. U.D.Ex. W.D.C. of Merit
Ceilidh	Heldrews Forgive 'N' Forget of Ardfern C.D.Ex. (October 1991 to not known)	*S.* Shercoz Gundo *D.* Heldrews Cleo
Tegan	Hazroh Dazzle C.D.Ex., U.D.Ex., W.D.Ex., T.D.C. of Merit, P.D.C. of Merit (October 1993 —)	*S.* Ch. Laios van Noort Sch.H.III, *D.* Hazroh Baby Boofuls

II Abbreviations Used in the Text

C.D.	Companion Dog
Ch.	Champion
Ex.	Excellent
GSD	German Shepherd Dog
Int.	International
Ob.	Obedience
P.D.	Patrol Dog (formerly Police Dog)
Sch.I, II, III	Schutzhund (Guard or Defence Dog)
T.D.	Tracker Dog
U.D.	Utility Dog
v.d.	von der
V Rated	Breed assessment (Very Good)
W.D.	Working Dog
W.T.	Working Trials

Index